Blurring the Boundaries

UNIVERSITIES *at* MEDWAY

RESEARCH *INTO* PRACTICE

RESEARCH *INTO* PRACTICE

Blurring the Boundaries

A fresh look at housing and care provision for older people

Christine Oldman

Published by:

Pavilion Publishing (Brighton) Ltd
8 St George's Place
Brighton, East Sussex BN1 4GB

Telephone: 01273 623222
Fax: 01273 625526
Email: pavpub@pavilion.co.uk
Website: www.pavpub.com

In association with:

Joseph Rowntree Foundation
The Homestead
40 Water End
York YO30 6WP

and

Norah Fry Research Centre
University of Bristol
3 Priory Road
Bristol BS8 1TX

First published 2000

Editor: Liz Mandeville
Cover and page design and layout: Stanford Douglas
Printing: Paterson Printing (Tunbridge Wells)

Blurring the Boundaries

The Joseph Rowntree Foundation has supported this project as part of its programme of research and innovative development projects, which it hopes will be of value to policy makers and practitioners. The facts presented and the views expressed in this report, however, are those of the authors and not necessarily those of the Foundation.

Contents

Acknowledgements

The Joseph Rowntree Foundation supported this research. I am grateful for their encouragement and especially for that provided by my advisory group of experts.

A number of people gave me a great deal of help and support during the course of the study. First and foremost I would like to thank the older people, and their relatives, whom I talked to. All were very willing to share experiences and, in some cases, to discuss difficult or sensitive issues. I would also like to thank the providers who were interviewed; like the 'consumers', they were very honest and very thoughtful about their services.

Introduction

This report is concerned with 'bricks and mortar' provision for older people which is neither unambiguously sheltered housing nor unambiguously residential care but falls somewhere in between.

Tinker (Royal Commission, 1999b Ch. 5) has commented that very sheltered housing, intended to be more care-orientated than 'ordinary' sheltered housing, has been established for around 20 years. However, this report is a response to more recent developments in service provision for older people which have resulted in housing-based models of care moving considerably up the policy agenda. The new century has seen a spate of conferences and publications about housing forms of provision for older people which, the protagonists claim, promote independence and dignity and reduce reliance on residential care. These new forms are variously called assisted living, close care, extra care housing, Category two-and-a-half or very sheltered housing.

The slow development of what Tinker calls 'very sheltered housing' over the last 20 years was very much a quiet activity, not much noticed by the social care community. It was led very largely by local authority housing departments and registered social landlords responding to difficulties posed by ageing populations of sheltered tenants. However, the recent revival in interest in provision for older people has involved social care professionals. In some areas of the country for example, the impetus for developments in the new hybrid forms of provision has come from social services departments faced with problems caused by old and outmoded local authority residential care homes. There have been other developments which have contributed to this recent interest in the potential of housing-based schemes to support frail older people. The publication of *With Respect to Old Age* (the report of the Royal Commission on the Funding of Long Term Care) in February 1999 renewed discussion about alternatives to institutional care. The Commission called for further expansion and development of innovative housing schemes. In addition, the Department of Health, with the White Paper *Modernising Social Services* (DoH, 1998a) and subsequent guidance, put considerable emphasis on prevention, independence and, by implication, alternatives to residential care.

The purpose of this report is to look systematically and analytically at the various forms of housing and care provision which have emerged over the years, and increasingly in the last five years or so, with the aim of providing some guidance to both providers and consumers. The once-sharp divide between 'housing' provision and 'care' provision has been breached; the models which have emerged conform to neither pure sheltered housing nor pure residential care. There is a fair amount of confusion for all involved as to what these variants are trying to achieve, how they compare in terms of both costs and effectiveness and how they are currently being affected by a changing policy environment.

Very sheltered housing was one of four alternatives[1] to residential care which the Royal Commission singled out for specialised study and comparative costing. The Age Concern Institute of Gerontology research team which was charged with the task of appraising these four models concluded that, despite the increased interest in very sheltered housing, very little is known either

---

[1] The other three were intensive home support, co-resident care and assistive technology.

about the quality of care provided within schemes or about outcomes. Indeed, although there have been a number of recent 'evaluations' of these hybrid forms over the last few years or so, they have generally been very much producer/provider-led and must inevitably be judged as such. The main omission in these attempts to comment on and appraise the newer forms of provision has been a strong and credible user perspective. Although, as will be shown below, some reports do contain tenant satisfaction surveys, generally older people have not in any fundamental sense been active participants in debates about different living arrangements in later life.

What this report offers is not a comprehensive evaluation of the different ways of supporting people with care needs in housing schemes. There is simply, as yet, a lack of consensus about how this should be done. Rather, the report hopes to inform discussion about how alternative living arrangements for older people who need support and care can be judged and appraised. It also aims to stimulate a wider debate about the future of bricks and mortar provision for older people.

Outline of the report

The report begins by describing the study's policy context. It summarises key contemporary issues in both residential care and sheltered housing and it offers an explanation for the apparent blurring of the boundaries between the two. It analyses the breaking up of what has traditionally been called the housing and care divide, locates the new 'prevention' agenda within these developments and looks at models of later life which underpin service delivery in both the housing and care sectors. There then follows an overview of the main models of providing housing and care which have emerged recently: their purpose, organisational structures, costs, entry issues, physical design and service delivery. **Chapter Five** focuses on evaluation and a pilot approach is offered by reference to initiatives in the Centre for Housing Policy's home town, York. The report concludes with a look at the future of housing and care provision in the light of policy uncertainties.

How the study was carried out

The study was carried out over seven months during 1999/2000. It also drew on earlier work carried out by the Centre for Housing Policy in the area of housing and care provision for older people. The following have been drawn upon: an evaluation of Joseph Rowntree Housing Trust's initiative known as 'flexi-care' (Oldman & Pleace, 1993; Oldman & Pleace, 1995; Oldman, 1998), an evaluation of all Anchor Trust's housing with care schemes (Oldman *et al*, 1997; Oldman & Quilgars, 1999) and a study of the role of relatives in sheltered housing (England *et al*, 2000).

There were three components to the study:

- literature review
- semi-structured telephone interviews with selected providers and other 'key players' (see **Appendix A**)
- case study 'pilot' evaluations of two innovations: Joseph Rowntree's flexi-care scheme and the City of York's supported housing schemes, which both involved qualitative fieldwork with older people, relatives, managers and care staff, and are described in the report.

Terminology

Everyone uses terms differently and interchangeably; there is no consensus as to what precisely 'very sheltered', 'extra care,' 'assisted living' etc, are. In order that this report 'flow', a decision has been made to opt for one phrase throughout – 'very sheltered housing' – to refer to all the different models which are discussed. However, the conclusion recommends that all these different labels be consigned to a lexicon scrap heap and the term 'supported housing' substituted.

Chapter One
The policy environment

Two forms of provision for older people exist in Britain, which operate within quite distinct policy and funding frameworks. One is residential care, which is subject to a strict care regulatory and inspection framework and where residents have no security of tenure and are not eligible for 'in the community' social security benefits. The other is sheltered housing, which is outside the care regulatory framework and where occupants are tenants with housing rights and eligibility for Housing Benefit and related benefits. Both, however, increasingly have a common purpose, and sheltered housing tenants may be as frail or disabled as those living in residential care.

In the past, there was clarity about what residential care was and what sheltered housing was. Although both are examples of communal living in that both have varying degrees of communal or public space and/or sharing of facilities, the boundaries were quite distinct. Residential care has been seen as dependent living and sheltered housing as independent living. Fundamental to housing provision is the notion of 'your own front door'. Occupants, as householders, have housing rights, and care and support is largely an add-on. With residential care provision, the degree of communal living and sharing is greater. Care is an integral element.

Residential homes have been portrayed as exemplary of institutional life. Institutional care is where individuals spend the bulk of their sleeping and waking time in a setting which is not their home (Higgins, 1989). Higgins proposed an institution/home dichotomy (see *Table 1.1*, overleaf). It is a useful 'ideal type' against which different living arrangements for older people can be evaluated. In the model the characteristics of home and institution are polar: for example, public/private space and the strangeness of people/familiarity of people.

Higgins herself did not position sheltered housing in the right-hand side of her table; for her it possessed some of the characteristics of an institution. However, quite clearly, the various forms of sheltered housing do not easily fit into the left-hand side either. A central purpose of this report is to explore the extent to which the various forms of very sheltered housing are quasi-institution or quasi-home.

It became evident during this study that the recent emergence of forms of sheltered housing provision which feel neither like 'at home' nor like 'in a home' is, in the main, a response to organisational and management problems and the availability of funding, rather than arising out of any robust or serious study of what older people might

Table 1.1 The key characteristics of institutions and home	
Institutions	**Home**
Public space, limitations in privacy	Private space but may be some limitations in privacy
Living with strangers, rarely alone	May live alone or with relatives or friends, rarely with strangers
Staffed by professionals or volunteers	Normally no staff there but they may visit to provide services
Formal and lacking in intimacy	Informal and intimate
Sexual relationships discouraged	Sexual relationships (between certain family members) accepted
Owned, rented by other agencies	Owned and rented by inhabitants
Variations in size but may be large (in terms of physical space and number living there)	Variations in size but usually small
Limitations on choice and on personal freedom	Ability to exercise choice and considerable degree of freedom
Strangeness (of people, place, etc)	Familiarity (of people, place, etc)
Batch or communal living	Individual arrangements for eating, sleeping, leisure activities which can vary according to time and place

Source: Higgins (1989)

want. The focus of this report is to redress the balance.

Before we look more closely at what appears to be a convergence of the boundaries between residential and sheltered provision, the key policy issues affecting both are summarised (see ***Table 1.1***, above).

Residential care: issues and trends

The present system of residential care evolves directly from the Poor Law traditions of the nineteenth and early twentieth centuries. The opportunity espoused by Beveridge and Bevan immediately after the war to provide a comfortable, attractive 'hotel model' of provision was never implemented. The local authority home was set up by the *National Assistance Act 1948*. Section 21 stated that it shall be the duty of every local authority to provide residential accommodation for persons who:

'by reasons of age, infirmity or any other circumstances are in need of care or attention which is not otherwise available'.

Although since the 1950s policy rhetoric has stressed the desirability of supporting older people in their own homes, there was very little progress made towards developing community care alternatives to residential care. The latter received an unintentional massive fillip in the 1980s, with the changes to the social assistance scheme allowing older people to enter private and voluntary sector (not local authority) residential care without any assessment of their need but solely on the basis of financial situation. A dramatic increase in residents of independent sector homes resulted.

The principal purpose of the *1990 NHS and Community Care Act* was to remove the 'perverse incentive' in favour of residential care. It has only been partly successful. As soon as weekly home care costs social services more than a week's residential care, a move into care becomes likely. Charging frameworks take into account the capital released from the sale of an older person's property when they enter residential care, and a residential allowance is available from the Government to fund individuals in private and voluntary nursing and residential homes. Increasing numbers of older people are home-owners. As a result, in nearly all situations it is substantially cheaper for local authorities to place people in residential care, even where there is no difference between the gross cost of residential care and care at home (Audit Commission, 1996). Between 1970 and 1998 the overall number of residential care, nursing home and NHS long-stay places in the UK has more than doubled, but the balance of provision has shifted dramatically in that period, with local authority and NHS long-stay provision falling sharply, private residential care growing constantly and nursing homes being the fastest-growing sector.

Demand and need are problematic concepts as far as residential care is concerned. There is no agreed dependency level at which entry to a care home is assumed appropriate. There are a range of factors determining why one person goes into a home and another does not. It is, for example, often observed that having a spouse is one of the most important factors keeping people out of care homes (Laing & Buisson, 1998). Care needs are a factor, but only one. Inappropriate housing may be a factor contributing to admission (Royal Commission, 1999b). Netten *et al* (1998) found that nearly half of all residents had low dependency, 16% had moderate dependency, 18% had severe dependency and 20% had total dependency.[1]

Almost universally, the UK literature compares living *in* a home unfavourably with living *at* home. Residential care is generally regarded by policy makers, providers and older people as the provision of last resort. Emotive language can be used – '*older people face residential care with fear and loathing*' (Peace *et al*, 1997) – and there is considerable discussion in both policy and practice literature about how to identify and manage those people at the 'margins' of residential care, those 'at risk' of going into residential care. Living at home, by contrast, is equated with privacy, informality, freedom and familiarity.

'*Older people are still wary. We have argued that this wariness is justified in so far as residential settings still represent a threat – not to individuality but much more profoundly to self*' (Peace *et al*, 1997).

Peace *et al* acknowledges that some residential care has tried to take on the characteristics of domestic environments, in response to concerns during the 1980s and 1990s about low standards and the depersonalising effects of institutional living. Anchor Trust, for example, although it has now dropped the label, called its residential homes 'housing with care'. The concept of 'your own front door' is incorporated into the design of its schemes. Each resident, typically, has their own flatlet, each with its own letterbox. Principles of privacy seem to be well-enshrined in care delivery (Oldman *et al*, 1997). Some limited cooking facilities are given to people and space standards are more generous than conventional residential care.

So, although, as we shall see, much of the present blurring of boundaries between

---

[1] Barthel index of activities of daily living (grouped).

housing and care provision comes from the housing end of service provision, it comes also from the care end. Residential care itself is changing and trying to become more like housing. There are a number of examples other than that of Anchor Trust's provision (above). Clough (1997), once an impassioned advocate of high-quality residential care, now argues for a substitution of residential care in its entirety by specialised housing schemes where people rent or own their living space and care is delivered to them. There is increasingly a view that residential care is outdated, unlikely to survive in the long term, and replaceable by housing models (for example, see the Association of Directors of Social Services' evidence to the Royal Commission). This emerging interest by social care professionals in housing provision has a pragmatic edge. Social services senior staff have recently become converted to the potential of housing resources. Pressure on care budgets and difficulties caused by the high revenue costs and declining quality of much Part III provision has prompted attention to sheltered housing.

The unpopularity of residential care has a down side. In Britain, collective living arrangements are viewed very negatively. The move to a residential home is viewed as a failure. It is also almost exclusively cast in care terms; a move to a home is considered necessary when informal care arrangements have broken down or if it is considered that care needs have increased to such a level that it is uneconomic to support the person in their own home. It is rarely acknowledged that some people may prefer to move to a quality environment where they can derive benefits from living with others from a similar generation. Rummery and Glendinning (1999) have pointed out that the new funding system for residential and nursing care has reduced the rights of people to gain entry to such provision.

The system of regulation of social care in this country is being radically changed via the *Care Standards Act 2000* which comes into force in 2002. At the time of writing, private and voluntary residential and nursing homes must be registered under the *1984 Residential Homes Act* (*RHA*). If an establishment is providing personal care and meals, it is obliged to register under the RHA and then falls under the responsibilities of the social care regulatory authorities. Under the new arrangements, registration, inspection and enforcement will be extended to local authorities' own care homes and statutory regulation of domiciliary care introduced for the first time. The new National Care Standards Commission will be established to take over the regulation of care services from individual local and health authorities.

The Royal Commission was enormously influential in drawing attention to the current issues bedevilling care provision. Those who move into residential or nursing care commonly do so in their mid-80s onwards, often after the trauma of an admission to hospital or a period of living at home with care services. There is a great deal of concern and anxiety about the funding arrangements, which are perceived to be unfair. Many older people believe they are made to pay twice, once through the national insurance system, which they thought would pay for their needs in later life, and again out of their assets. Older people who own their own property have to use their assets to pay for their care. Those who are funded by the state are left with only a small sum as 'pocket money'. The inequity between free NHS care and social care, for which charges are levied, is a growing concern, with the withdrawal of long-term care from the NHS. If an older person has cancer they will receive care free at the point of consumption; if they suffer from Alzheimer's they might be paying in excess of £350 a week in a nursing home.

The current funding system provides no incentive to local authorities to provide domiciliary care. The system appears to be designed around a series of different bureaucracies, rather than the needs of individual older people. The Royal Commission's central recommendation, namely that personal care – whether delivered in *a* home or *at* home – should be funded out of general taxation, has not been accepted by the Government. Its response to the Commission contained in the NHS Plan, July 2000, falls far short of what many were hoping for. Only nursing costs in care homes will be free at the point of consumption.

Sheltered housing: issues and trends

Sheltered housing goes back a long way, as far as the 1950s (Butler *et al*, *ibid*), and shortly after, some time in the 1960s, the debate began on whether it was meeting housing need or care need (Butler *et al*, 1983). At this point, sheltered housing was quite clearly seen as an alternative to the sort of demeaning and sometimes abusive residential care which Peter Townsend (1962) was so effectively inveighing against in his famous study, *The Last Refuge*. At the same time, local authority housing departments saw the development of sheltered housing as an opportunity to address their general housing responsibilities. At a time of housing need, older people were seen as under-occupying council houses which were sorely needed for families. If older people could be attracted by the offer of small, purpose-built, manageable accommodation with some support, a larger housing problem could be solved. In the 1970s, as public expenditure crises loomed, sheltered housing gained even more in popularity as it became increasingly apparent that residential care was expensive and being used for significant numbers of older people who did not need it

(Plank, 1977; Neill *et al*, 1988). The concept of the continuum of care held sway at this time, and policy analysts were enjoined to take on the task of devising resource-allocation models which would ensure that people moved to a more intensive stage when a specified level of dependency had been reached.

From the early 1980s, sheltered housing attracted some criticism from academics. Butler *et al* (1983) cited a warden from their fieldwork to illustrate the housing/care tension inherent in sheltered housing:

> *'If you are independent, sheltered housing is an over-provision; if you are dependent, it is an under-provision.'*

They also questioned some of the claims made by providers of sheltered housing, including the claim that it 'prolonged' life. Laura Middleton (1981) employed the epithet '*so much for so few*'. Middleton was critical of the segregation from the rest of the community which she believed the provision embodied. It was a myth, she claimed, that it helped maintain independent living when it involved moving to a community under surveillance.

In a similar vein, Clapham and various colleagues have condemned sheltered housing on the grounds that it is 'special needs' and stigmatising. Clapham and Munro (1988) argued for sheltered housing resources to be made available to the wider community in which they are located. Clapham has argued that sheltered housing was ill thought out and over-provided and should be brought fully into the mainstream of community care, through upgrading to very sheltered standards (Clapham, 1997; Clapham & Munro, 1990).

During the 1980s and 1990s, sheltered housing providers began to address the various management problems that they were then facing. Tenant populations were ageing and morbidity levels increasing. The limited facilities of sheltered housing provided insufficient support and domiciliary care was often unavailable or inadequate. Wardens complained that they were subject to severe work pressures. At this time the provision was generally not claiming to provide a 'home for life'. There was evidence (McCafferty, 1994; Royal Commission, 1999b) that moves to residential care from sheltered housing were greater than for equivalent populations living in mainstream housing. Providers were able to access, on behalf of their tenants, the entitlement-based, means-tested residential care allowance. As well as this, on-site wardens were able to exert some pressure locally to achieve a move for tenants who were making their jobs burdensome. After the changes to the funding of residential care in April 1993, it became harder to move tenants to residential care, because social services had to be persuaded of the need. Also, despite the alleged expansion of home care, the problem of obtaining adequate domiciliary care for tenants continued (Thompson & Page, 1999).

Gradually, very sheltered housing began to emerge as a response to the above issues. Although there is much argument over definitions, the latter is broadly distinguishable from 'ordinary' sheltered housing by:

- the provision of a meal
- the provision of additional services
- the possibility of a more barrier-free environment.

In other words, these features are added to or modify the basic building blocks of ordinary sheltered housing: a resident warden who contractually cannot offer domestic help or personal care, (usually) some communal areas, and an alarm system.

A further spur to the development of these newer forms of provision was that of

'difficult to let' sheltered housing. In 1994 eight per cent of local authorities and thirteen per cent of housing associations had over half their stock designated as difficult to let. Tinker *et al*'s (1995) explanations for this phenomenon were:

- undesirable locations
- accommodation that was too small, including unpopular bedsits
- sharing of some facilities and lack of facilities such as lifts.

Other commentators (Marsh & Riseborough, 1995; Nocon & Pleace, 1999; Oldman, 1991) have suggested that the perception that high rents and service charges are not giving value for money is a further reason for the difficulty some providers have had in filling schemes. Concerned to address the problem of voids, providers in the 1990s began to look at remodelling schemes where demand was slow, and started to create more supportive environments.

By the 1990s, sheltered housing was falling out of favour with policy makers, in part because of the Government's commitment to 'new' community care principles and in part because of pressures to reduce public expenditure. The strong message from several quarters, starting with the White Paper *Caring for People* (Department of Health, 1989), was that older people should be supported in their own, existing, homes where, it was stated, they preferred to be. The thinking became concerned with bringing support services *to* people, not moving them to specialist provision, be it care or housing. The idea of 'moving on' along a continuum of care had, in theory at least, been challenged. Sheltered housing providers were encouraged to help their tenants maintain their tenancies. Initiatives such as Care and Repair were marketed at the expense of moving options. The negative attitude to residential care began to spread to special needs housing. Cooper *et al* (1994) commented:

> 'The image of shared housing has…
> suffered from the declining importance
> attached to the idea of communality and
> the growing emphasis on independent
> living and personal autonomy as the
> central goal of supported housing'
> (1994).

Also in the 1990s, the Department of Environment's influential study of the housing needs of elderly and disabled people, *Living Independently* (McCafferty, 1994), highlighted the lack of care and support within ordinary sheltered housing. It was critical of the fact that provision was accommodating high levels of low dependency. A key finding was that a high proportion of recent entrants (41% of ordinary sheltered housing tenants and 22% of very sheltered housing tenants) had no physical or mental dependency. The Audit Commission added to this analysis of ordinary sheltered housing in its report *Home Alone* (1998).

> 'The principle of community care makes
> it harder to justify tying resources to
> property rather than people. Sheltered
> housing must accordingly re-invent itself
> as provision for older people who prefer
> the presence of a supportive community,
> or it must re-think the levels of need it is
> able to support. If it does not, it will face
> serious questions about its relevance in a
> system which can deliver high levels of
> support in ordinary housing' (1998).

These re-appraisals resulted in the decline in capital subsidies available for specialised housing provision for older people. The supply of sheltered housing, as measured by new completions, fell dramatically in the local authority, housing association and private sectors alike. In 1997 only 402 units of sheltered housing were built in England (Royal Commission, 1999b, Ch. 5 Table 5.2).

The last policy development affecting housing provision for older people is *Supporting People* (Department of Social Security, 1998). In 2003 a new policy and funding framework for supported housing and support services will be introduced. The current entitlement-based, demand-led system will be replaced by a system redolent of the community care arrangements. Currently, Housing Benefit is a key ingredient of supported and sheltered housing finance. It covers much of the support costs of sheltered housing. The development of very sheltered projects has been made possible by the availability of this and other housing finance. In 2003 the social security system will cover only the bricks and mortar component of sheltered and supported housing rents. The support element will be paid for out of strictly cash-limited grants administered by local authorities. The thinking underpinning Supporting People is similar to that noted above in the discussion on current policies towards sheltered housing. The proposals aim to encourage the development of support services to vulnerable people living in ordinary housing as an alternative to special needs housing. Whether Supporting People represents a threat or an opportunity to the new forms of housing and care provision for older people will be discussed later on in the report.

The breaking up of the housing and community care divide

It will be apparent from the above that, before the implementation of the new community care in 1993, housing was far from being integrated into community care policies. Although housing need is by no means as central to community care as many believe it should be, the traditional divide between housing and care has been breached. Fletcher *et al* (1999) argued that the development of very sheltered housing is a response to a quite recent and, in their view, an overdue strategic approach on the part of local authorities to older people's service provision.

During the 1990s local authorities have, very slowly, developed community care strategies which embrace, to a greater or lesser degree, housing provision and which call for a clearer community care role for sheltered housing. There is evidence, Fletcher *et al* asserts, of a new 'whole systems' approach to service provision for older people, involving housing, health and social services. A few local authorities are looking to reconfigure their services to older people, and housing forms a key part of this process. Joint working between agencies is an essential part of this new thinking and, although it continues to work imperfectly, a number of new initiatives such as Joint Investment Plans (Department of Health, 1998b) and Partnership in Action (Department of Health, 1998c) place a great deal of emphasis on specific examples of joint working, such as joint assessment and commissioning. Finally, the *Health Act 1999* gave, from April 2000, all principal local authorities, health authorities, NHS trusts and primary care trusts the power to pool budgets and resources, introduce lead commissioning and establish integral provision.

Housing also forms part of the new prevention agenda. The Social Services White Paper *Modernising Social Services* (Department of Health, 1998a) heralded a new approach to the delivery of community care, one that tries to move away from targeting intensive home care services to small groups of highly dependent users, to an approach that delivers preventative and rehabilitative services. Increasingly it was being realised that some residential care admissions

might have been avoided if preventative, recuperative and rehabilitative schemes had existed. Within health policy as well there has been a new focus on prevention and the promotion of wellbeing, with the advent of health improvement programmes and health action zones. Crucially, as far as the development of new forms of housing and care provision for older people is concerned, funding systems are being changed with the intention of taking 'perverse incentives' out of the system and reducing funding fragmentation and complexity. Specific 'pots' of money include:

- £647 million over three years for the partnership grant for rehabilitation and intermediate services

- £100 million over three years to promote preventative initiatives.

However, housing is not, as yet, as central to the prevention agenda as it might be. Age Concern (1998) noted that *Modernising Social Services* contained no explicit mention of the potential for sheltered housing to play a more central role in community care provision and of the need for social services departments to work in conjunction with housing providers to develop alternatives to residential care. The reconfiguration of older people's services, remarked upon by Fletcher *et al* (1999), by those local authorities which are thinking more strategically about older people's services is arguably carried out more in the interests of achieving greater cost-effective-ness than in a spirit of genuine understanding of the importance of housing in older people's health and wellbeing. Housing professionals would argue that they have been part of an implicit prevention agenda for very many years and, as we shall see later in this report, claims are made that good quality, supportive housing environments can obviate the need for expensive and unpopular institutional care. But in a detailed two-year study

Harrison and Heywood (2000) have fairly conclusively shown that local planning systems consistently fail either to quantify the bad impact of some housing environments on the health of older people or to make provision to meet that need.

Service delivery and models of later life

Traditionally, older people have been viewed as passive beneficiaries of services delivered to them. For many years the discussion was in terms of the 'problem' of the elderly, and there was a hint of moral panic about the economic and social implications of an ageing population. However, there is some evidence that the language at least has changed. Issues concerning older people are now high on the policy agenda. Older people are being recognised as major stakeholders in society. The Labour administration, on taking office in 1997, set up an interministerial group on older people's issues, with the aim of connecting up government departmental policies. Gradually, older people are being recognised in social exclusion debates which very much began by focusing on welfare-to-work issues. The Royal Commission on the Funding of Long Term Care has itself played an important part in criticising, in a very trenchant manner, the dependency model which informed service delivery. At the local level, interagency issues are the focus of the Better Government for Older People projects which promote citizenship and involvement by older people in their local communities. A further important breakthrough in the tendency to discriminate against older people in service provision is the agreement not to debar the latter any more from the provisions of the *1996 Direct Payments Act*. It is now possible for people aged 65 or over to be given cash with which they can buy the care and support services they want.

There is also a new emphasis on quality and raising of standards. It has already been noted that a new form of regulation for residential, nursing and domiciliary care for all 'vulnerable' groups is in the process of being implemented. The *Care Standards Act* has repealed the *Residential Homes Act* and put a new system in place, and in 1999 the Government published *Fit for the Future?* (Department of Health, 1999), a consultation paper on nationally required standards for residential and nursing care for older people which will ensure consistent standards throughout the country. In addition, the National Service Frameworks, the Long Term Care Charter and *Better Services for Vulnerable People* (Department of Health, 1997) are all other examples of initiatives which are intended to contribute to the raising of standards and consistency of service delivery throughout the country. The introduction of the Best Value framework is relevant here as well. Best Value, replacing Competitive Compulsory Tendering, requires that local authorities and other publicly funded agencies subject all their services to a fundamental review of cost and quality over a maximum five-year period.

Fletcher and colleagues (1999), in their account of the emergence of very sheltered housing, argue that the new developments arise out of a sea-change in how older people are viewed. They argue that local authorities are beginning to commission very sheltered housing out of a new concern to see older people as citizens, not passive beneficiaries of welfare. Fletcher and his colleagues feel there is a growing recognition that older people demand to be 'socially included' and to live independent lives in the community.

In this report a rather less sanguine view is taken of this alleged conversion by welfare practitioners. While it is undoubtedly true that the language has moved away from an approach which focuses on the problems of a growing and dependent group, the study has found little evidence that the recent developments are based on sustained dialogue with older people themselves. Sheltered housing has always been considered separately from the rest of the supported housing movement, and indeed, policy and funding frameworks are different. Concepts derived from the independent living movement, such as empowerment and choice, are not yet common currency in debates on housing provision for older people. For instance, the report will provide evidence that service delivery is still framed within a medical rather than a social model of disability.

Conclusions

Although very sheltered housing has been around for some considerable time, interest in it as a possibly radical form of provision for older people is relatively new. Strong claims have been made in some quarters that very sheltered housing, with its central concept of 'your own front door', can replace traditional residential care. Currently, two different forms of communal living for older people exist side by side, the one, residential care, subject to regulation and inspection and the other, sheltered housing, which, although affected by housing regulatory frameworks, does not have to account in a rigorous way for the care and support it provides. Moreover, outcomes for the two sets of residents are likely, in terms of disposable income at least, to be different. While the full range of community benefits are available to the sheltered housing resident, the older person living in a care home is not eligible for Housing Benefit. However, the two settings are growing closer

in what they aim to do and whom they accommodate.

Residential care in Britain is regarded as the provision of last resort. Despite the community care legislation, a bias towards institutional settings and against 'at home' solutions for very dependent older people continues. There is considerable public disquiet about the apparent unfairness of the funding system. Sheltered housing has fallen out of favour with policy makers, although there is support for a clear community care role for the provision. Generally, there is a lack of enthusiasm in Britain on the part of those who influence policy for collective living arrangements, whether they are care- or housing-based. They are seen as an economic necessity when informal care arrangements are failing to work.

Some residential care has begun to look a little more like housing, and sheltered housing has come to look a little more like residential care, for a number of reasons. Social care providers, aware of the unpopularity of much residential care, are looking to substitute housing forms of provision for what is perceived to be more expensive local authority residential care provision. Sheltered housing providers increasingly face problems with traditional schemes; they cannot obtain adequate domiciliary care for their more frail tenants, they cannot access residential care as easily as they did in the past and they have some difficulty letting some schemes. Finally, the new community care is about bringing support to people, not moving them to increasingly supportive environments. Very sheltered housing is symbolic of the new preventative and rehabilitative community care agenda.

Chapter Two

The new models: purposes and organisational structures

Although there is some uncertainty as to what is being included in published estimates we can be sure that very sheltered housing is numerically quite small. Latest figures show there are around half a million sheltered units in England but only 23,000 (5%) of them are very sheltered. All the evidence, however, is that this statistic is increasing quite rapidly.

Nearly all very sheltered units are found in the social rented sector. Laing and Buisson (1998) report that, of the total of around 21,000 sheltered units in the private sector, only a very small number could be designated as 'very sheltered'. However, all the predictions appear to be that this will change in the near future as the sector begins to realise the market opportunities afforded by an ageing population of home owners. The figures in **Table 2.1**, below, show that registered social landlords (housing associations) have a

higher proportion (9.5% compared with 2.5%) of very sheltered stock than local authorities.

It became apparent in the course of the research that, despite the paucity of this type of provision, there was considerable variety in the forms adopted, in terms of the aims of the provision, the size and physical design, funding mechanisms, care and support services delivery patterns and so on. The aims of this and the next two chapters are to look for patterns and to identify the most important features which distinguish schemes.

What is very sheltered housing for?

Home for life?

Central to the concept of very sheltered housing is that 'moving on' should be minimised. However, how this aim is operationalised varies. Very few providers in the study admitted to an explicit or unambiguous policy of providing a 'home for life' but all were committed to the idea of 'ageing in place'. Some providers were against the provision of very sheltered housing as a

Table 2.1	Very sheltered housing provision in England, 1998
	Number of units
Local authority	
sheltered	274,868
very sheltered	7,100
Housing associations	
sheltered	166,774
very sheltered	15,817
Total	**464,559**

Source: HIP returns; CORE and supported CORE data

specialised built form but, rather, aimed to provide ageing in place through adaptation of ordinary sheltered housing so that it might serve as a less disabling environment and/or through the introduction of support services to people when the need arose. To some extent, of course, ageing in place now happens by default. All sheltered housing providers face problems in obtaining adequate social services help for their clients and/or of getting the latter to fund the care costs of a person whom the provider believes needs residential care. However, solutions to these problems differ.

Anchor Trust, for example, was associated with an 'ordinary housing' approach and it pioneered in Newcastle (Gibbs & Wright, 1993) the provision of an in-house home care team, funded at the time from joint finance, which supported tenants when the need arose. Such an approach was defended in terms of its non-stigmatising approach to the needs of older people. Avoiding constructing a specialised built environment better protected the housing feel of a scheme and, it was argued, was in line with community care principles of delivering services *to* people and not the reverse. Anchor has continued with this policy and, through its subsidiary, Anchor Care Alternatives, has expanded the model to other parts of the country where care teams support both tenants and older people living in ordinary housing in the vicinity of schemes. This 'ordinary housing' approach needs to be judged alongside a provider's allocation policies. Many providers have reviewed these in recent years and are less likely to allocate tenancies solely on housing need; subsequently, the necessity to evolve ageing-in-place strategies becomes more compelling as tenants become iller or more disabled rather earlier than they might have done in the past. More recently, Anchor has adopted an eclectic approach and has added extra

care housing to its already quite extensive portfolio of housing and care services. It now categorises 26 of its schemes as extra care, but still emphasises the ordinariness of these settings. In these schemes care and support services are available to all the tenants.

Remodelling

A rather different approach to the issue of providing a home for life or of making a reality of the rather less stringent objective, ageing in place, is a re-invention of traditional sheltered housing through remodelling. Ordinary sheltered housing, given its purpose of meeting the housing needs of older people, is remarkably non-barrier-free. Many schemes do not have lifts, doorways will not accommodate wheelchairs and kitchens are difficult for people with arthritis. Remodelling also sometimes arises as a response to problems created by low-demand bedsit schemes. It can be minimal – the refurbishing of two or three units in a scheme – or extensive – involving the recasting of an entire scheme. Remodelling does not simply involve physical modifications but, equally crucially, the re-skilling of staff so they can provide flexible support services (Phillips, 1998). Housing 21 is the provider which has been the most associated with remodelling (Trotter & Phillips, 1997). Its aim is to offer older people a wider choice; the emphasis is more on preventative provision rather than on directly diverting people from residential care.

Re-inventing residential care

Fletcher *et al* (1999) argues that the models described above are re-inventions of traditional sheltered housing and derive principally from housing routes. A rather different approach to the issue of a home for life is that adopted by those schemes which owe their origins more to strong partnerships with the social care sector. Fletcher describes this variant of sheltered housing as de-institutionalisation or the re-invention of residential care. It aims to divert from residential care and be an alternative to it. Implied in these statements of intent is the assertion that very sheltered housing is a cheaper alternative to residential care and even intensive domiciliary care. The well publicised initiative by Wolverhampton to replace its local authority residential care provision with very sheltered housing is a clear example of this model (Bailey, 1998). Similarly, East Leigh District Council in Hampshire, now a voluntary stock transfer, has received some media attention for its belief that very sheltered housing renders residential care obsolete. Fletcher *et al* (1999) catalogues a number of local authorities which have or are commissioning very sheltered housing to replace or supplement residential provision. The exact number is not known.

The issue of a home for life is largely taken care of in these models because, in some versions at least, those who are allocated tenancies are people who would be described as being on the margins of residential care and who would in other circumstances have been admitted to residential care. How close an alternative to residential care these schemes are varies. At the extreme end, they represent an attempt by hard-pressed social services departments to transfer their budgetary problems over to a housing arena. The regimes that are operated may seem very little different from those they replace: ie ordinary residential care. By contrast, the dozen or so extra care schemes that Hanover Housing Association runs aim to provide something which is capable of diverting from residential care but is quite different in terms of the service which is offered.

Greenwood and Smith, in their evaluation of Hanover's extraCare schemes, comment:

'There is every sign that extraCare is capable of evolving into a realistic alternative to the care provided in residential or nursing homes for the great majority of older people needing some form of grouped provision. It has the great advantage of not carrying the stigma of an institution, of making possible a greater degree of independence and self-determination and offering older people much more generous private space as a basis for the fulfilment of all the other rights individuals should be able to enjoy' (Greenwood & Smith, 1999).

Hanover, and other schemes which fall into the re-invention of residential care category, tend to be new-built.

Mixed sites

There are a growing number of sites around the country where the issue of a home for life is resolved by providing different facilities: bungalows, residential and nursing care on the same site. Hartrigg Oaks (see below) and Red Lodge (the York case study, see **Chapter Five**) are examples.

Home for life: a problematic notion

The extent to which 'home for life' is a central aim or is made explicit and transparent differs from model to model. Some models, such as Joseph Rowntree Housing Trust's (JRHT) retirement village in New Earswick near York, is exemplary of those to whom it is a central aim; it is included in its description – Hartrigg Oaks: continuing care community. Both JRHT and the ExtraCare Charitable Trust's retirement village at Berryhill, Stoke-on-Trent aim to provide care up to and including nursing care. The difference between the two schemes is that, when over 21 hours of care is required by a JRHT resident, a move may be required to the on-site care facility. At Berryhill, and in ECCT's other schemes, care is delivered to the tenant or owner's flat. However, most providers believed that very sheltered housing could to some extent replace residential care but nursing care would continue to be absolutely necessary. The difficulty here, of course, is that in recent years not only have the boundaries between sheltered housing and residential care become blurred, but also those between residential and nursing care.

It was apparent from the study that the issue of a home for life is problematic and needs considerable clarification. In most non-registered schemes residents are assured tenants and hence have security of tenure. However, movement to residential and nursing care was evident in many of the schemes included in the study. It was not always clear in what circumstances this was happening and who was the key decision-maker: landlord, GP or other health professional, older person or family member. One provider, who was largely typical of those approached in this study response, said:

> *'There is no general rule about this.*
> *We have to look at each individual's*
> *circumstances. We can't give a pat answer.*
> *If they started to be a danger to those*
> *around them or themselves we would*
> *have a problem'.*

Providers talked about the relative claims of the individual and other residents. Dementia presented the chief difficulty to managers. Where the lives of other residents were perceived to be adversely affected by the behaviour or actions of someone with a dementia condition, a move to nursing or residential care was often strongly encouraged.

Explicit policies on home for life seemed largely absent, and residents and their relatives, it will be shown, were unclear as to the position on 'moving on'. Legally, landlords can evict tenants with assured tenancies, but they are required to make alternative living arrangements. In practice, it appears that recourse to the law is very rare; typically, all involved will accept the necessity for a move.

A better quality of life?

Some models, whether they have housing or social care origins, purport to offer benefits over and above a commitment to reducing the likelihood of a move to a more intensive environment. Some, indeed, aim to be able to give a better quality of life than would have been experienced in either residential care or the older person's own home. Two examples of providers which stress both quality of life and lifestyle are Extra Care Charitable Trust and Joseph Rowntree Housing Trust. Both aim to provide extensive facilities and stimulating environments which include a wide range of cultural, sporting and social activity. Some providers stress the preventative and/or rehabilitative role of their schemes. In this they are similar to the very early providers of sheltered housing, who argued quite fervently that a move to sheltered housing delayed dependency. Some schemes purport to rehabilitate, both in terms of reducing the amount of care a person has been receiving in the past and also in terms of providing an alternative form of accommodation for people who have previously been living in residential care. A very common theme with many of the variants is that of independence. By contrast with residential care, very sheltered housing claims to embody independent living. A counter to this claim is that it may be difficult for a scheme both to claim to be a close alternative to residential care and to provide a rehabilitative and preventative environment. However, very sheltered housing providers claim that their provision can arrest the dependency and decline associated with residential care.

A resource to the community

A brief mention needs to be made of a final purpose or aim of very sheltered housing. The main providers of very sheltered housing have all considered the deployment of some of very sheltered housing services to the wider community. There has been strong encouragement from the Audit Commission (1998) and the Department of Environment, Transport and the Regions (DETR) to extend what are regarded as costly resources beyond the boundaries of the scheme. A further justification is the breaking down of any boundaries there may be between the community and a specialist provision. Abbeyfield's interesting project near Seascale, Cumbria is such an example. As well as having both registered and non-registered units, the house accommodates a day centre which is used by older people who live outside as well as inside the house.

Organisational structures

Registered or non-registered

Whatever their aims, the different models have one thing in common: at the heart of very sheltered housing is the core concept of 'your own front door'. A great deal of store is set by the fact that older people have their own tenancies or leases. They have security of tenure and their rights are enshrined in housing law. Schemes are intended to feel more like 'living at home' than 'living in a home' (Oldman & Quilgars, 1999). However, one of the key factors which distinguishes the model is that some choose or are required, to be registered under the *Residential Homes Act*

(*RHA*). A central interest of this study is whether the 'housing' nature of a model is compromised if the scheme is registered.

At the time of writing, provision must be registered if the same organisation is providing both **personal care** and **board** and is **accommodating** one or more of the needs groups identified in the RHA. This requirement includes small projects of fewer than four people. The Act has been subject to local differences in interpretation. An identical very sheltered housing scheme might have been required to have been registered in one part of the country but not in another. If care is a condition of occupancy, or is provided by the same organisation which owns and manages the accommodation, registration may be required. Where care is charged for separately, and residents have a genuine choice of whether or not to receive it, registration is not usually expected. Some registration and inspection units will require registration if a certain level of care is being delivered. In the study, one provider told us that the a rule of thumb they encountered was 14 hours a week; if residents were receiving care above this level, the particular scheme would be registered. However, this practice seems fairly idiosyncratic and is not legally-based.

The *Care Standard Act 2000*'s registration requirements are much more in line with those currently operating in Scotland, where board is not a criterion. Instead, schemes must register if they are providing 'personal care'. Some attempt, not entirely successful in the view of some people consulted in the course of this study, has been made to define 'personal care'.

'For an establishment to count as a care home, it must provide assistance with bodily functions, where such assistance is required. It is very important to understand that that does not mean that the personal care provided by the home is

15

limited to assistance with bodily functions... the meaning of personal care is to be interpreted more widely than that. The amendment will simply mean that the type of assistance must be available and given if required. Clearly, the amount of such assistance that is given will depend on the needs of the residents. In a care home for the frail elderly people, it is likely to be given fairly often but in a care home for people with learning disabilities, it might be given only rarely. However, for an establishment to be registrable as a care home, assistance with bodily functions must be available even if it is rarely provided. The same requirement was contained in the Registered Homes Act 1984.' (John Hutton, Minister of State at the Department of Health)

Why is the issue of registration/non-registration of so much interest to this study? First, it appears to have some effect on the cost/quality relationship. Some providers interviewed during the research have resisted registration because they felt that its requirements add significantly to the costs of provision and do not contribute to its quality. Registration involves the costs of registering and the costs of meeting inspectors, require-ments regarding health and safety, staffing levels, etc. The new *Care Standards Act* may add to these costs through, for example, requiring training of staff, etc. There is a view widely held by those who are against registration that inspection focuses on inputs and not on those things which really measure the success of a project. These providers also said that quality is currently assessed in other ways and that that process will extend in the future. At present, where personal care is being delivered via arrangements with a local social services authority, contract compliance

ensures, in theory at least, that care is of a certain standard. Some providers in the study said that, in the future, quality would be further ensured, first through the requirement for any agency delivering domiciliary care to a scheme to be registered, and through the monitoring arrangements which local authorities will be required to carry out within the *Supporting People* framework. Ironically, at a time when they are being relieved of their care regulation responsibilities, local authorities have been given new duties to monitor support services.

The second reason the study focused on registration was to explore in some detail the concept of 'your own front door'. An occupant may have a licence or a tenancy but their concept of themselves as a householder living an independent life may be less secure if that front door is part of a registered stablishment. The environment may feel more 'institutional' than in a non-registered scheme. The concept of 'your own front door' goes far beyond housing issues. It refers to the ability to carry on with life as before, such as having grandchildren to sleep on the sofa, or inviting your friends in to watch television.

The third, and possibly most important, reason why the study paid some attention to the issue of registration relates to an unintended messy interaction between the RHA, the *NHS and Community Care Act 1990* and the social security system. An older person living in residential care entitled to financial support from the state with fees is left with £15.45[1] a week (2000–2001) as 'disposable income'. In a non-registered very sheltered scheme the same person has a higher disposable income because they are entitled to Housing Benefit and associated 'community' benefits (out of which the tenant has to pay for the living expenses which are included in a residential home fee). This

---

[1]Known as 'personal allowance'

disposable income issue, although very much a contentious one in other areas of supported housing, has received little attention in debates about housing provision for older people. Griffiths (1997) and Clapham *et al* (1994) have discussed the pauperisation effect of registration on occupants, and Simons (1998) has talked about the disempowering effects of reducing someone's income to personal allowance levels. In **Chapter Three** we explore the extent to which the older person living in a care home might be financially disadvantaged vis-à-vis their counterparts in non-registered very sheltered housing.

The difference between the two systems of provision – residential care and sheltered housing – is not simply one of different disposable incomes. It is more profound. The differences were described by one provider in this study as being the difference between a package holiday and making your own arrangements. In the residential care setting a blanket fee is paid which covers accommodation, care and living costs (with some important exceptions such as hairdressing, chiropody, incontinence pads). Although payment of these costs divides them into their separate parts, in terms of delivery it is a 'take it or leave it' approach. If someone's daughter still wants to give her mother a shower or take her bed linen home to be washed, or if a resident requires less or more care than the 'average', the system cannot respond. In the very sheltered housing setting the different components are charged for separately: rent and service charge, living costs and care costs. In theory, at least, there is some flexibility in the amount spent on food and other living costs and on care – the very sheltered housing tenant seems to be able to exercise more choice over their life.

Many providers aim to 'avoid' registration although, ironically, before the April 1993 changes in the funding of residential care,

housing schemes would purposefully seek registration in order to access the residential care allowance (Clapham *et al*, 1994). Even under the new arrangements, some providers feel that registration still delivers them financial advantage. A not-for-profit provider in Scotland has registered all the accommodation units in its village complex, including the self-contained flats.

In the study, respondents had quite different views about registration. Some providers were vehemently opposed.

> *'I would fight it [registration] tooth and nail. The inspector saying "I must look at your kitchen" completely makes a mockery of the idea of very sheltered housing being someone's own home.'*

> *'We think it [registration] does matter. We would not end up with a model that the resident thinks is a home. All residents have to accept risk.'*

This last comment implicitly refers to the reason why there is a large and complex regulatory machinery for establishments providing care. The *RHA* was introduced to give vulnerable people the protection from risk, abuse and just poor standards which had been a feature of such provision over the years. Some providers in the study believed that protection was very necessary, and two or three said they thought that service provision for frail older people had to be approached differently from provision for other groups. One provider said, '*We need the safeguard of regulation*'. Another provider felt strongly that the issue of registration could be something of a red herring. Principles of empowerment and independent living, they thought, were independent of legal definitions. Registered schemes were capable of being liberating environments. Equally, non-registered schemes could be disempowering and institutional in feel.

At the time of writing, the situation regarding very sheltered housing and the *Care Standards Act* remains unclear. Some people approached by the study felt that the current muddiness over what should be registered will remain. They said that it was disappointing that the Department of Health had not considered the question of regulation and inspection as far as housing schemes are concerned. An opportunity to sort out the anomaly of having the two systems side by side, one where residents have a much higher disposable income than in another, had been missed. The Audit Commission (1998) in its report *Home Alone* called for sheltered housing to be regulated, but at the same time drew attention to the financial plight of older people living in residential care. People in the study felt that the Government did not really intend that very sheltered housing *en masse* should be brought into the registration fold, but that it remains to be seen whether registration will be required in some circumstances. Certainly, with board taken out of the requirement to register, it seems likely that more very sheltered schemes than is currently the case, particularly those which provide night cover, will have to be registered. Although the Government has stated repeatedly that it does not want to see people's own homes registered as care homes, offering a tenancy does not exempt a home from registration as this could lead to the avoidance of registration by some providers.

Both registered and non-registered schemes were represented in the study. Interestingly, some organisations provided both registered and non-registered units in the same scheme. Indeed, this was the case in the pilot evaluation study reported on in **Chapter Five** as well as in Abbeyfield's project at Seascale in Cumbria.

Integration/separation of accommodation and care

Models can be distinguished as to whether the accommodation and care are provided by the same or different organisations. This issue very much links to the earlier one, discussed above, of whether provision should be registered. The essence of residential care is that accommodation and care come as a single package. A strong theme, however, in the new community care, is their separation. Local authority registration and inspection units are less likely to demand registration if accommodation and care are provided by different agencies. Within the supported housing movement there is generally a view that vulnerable people have a better chance of living empowered lives if their landlord and their care/support deliverers are different organisations. Schemes, it is argued, are more likely to feel like ordinary housing and less like residential care. Simons (1998) has noted that the key defining feature of residential care is not the provision of personal care, but the way in which the place a person lives is inextricably bound up with the help they receive. Simons' expertise lies largely in the field of learning disability. He argues that separating care from accommodation gives more control and power to residents/tenants. The latter can sack their care provider without fear of losing their accommodation. As far as provision for older people is concerned, the debate about whether accommodation and care should be separated is rarely conducted in these terms, but much more, as noted above, in terms of whether registration can be 'avoided' or by the perceived cost-effectiveness of the two different arrangements.

Hanover Housing Association quite deliberately chose to separate the provision of accommodation from the provision of care – partly, to avoid the necessity of registration. Hanover, with around ten very sheltered schemes in management, provides the 'bricks and mortar' with associated housing management services, and care is delivered to tenants by social services or by external care agencies under contract to their local authority. In each Hanover scheme there is an estate manager who has responsibility for it and provides what, in supported housing parlance, would be called **intensive housing management services**. The estate manager's role is similar to that of the traditional sheltered housing warden. The estate manager does not manage the care team. Hanover has shown very welcome candour in publishing the results of a consultancy by Greenwood and Smith (1999) which concluded that, in the early days, at least, of their experiment with extra care, the Hanover/social service partnership was sometimes problematic; in some schemes there were demarcation disputes between the estate manager and care workers as to who was responsible for what. Hanover currently has an open mind on the issue of integration/separation of accommodation and care. It speculated that, increasingly, social care commissioners will expect an integrated service. However, strong arguments were made by several respondents that the separation of accommodation and care is more congruent with community care principles.

Care delivered to the very sheltered housing scheme will come from the social services department or from a private or not-for-profit organisation working on its behalf. There is overwhelming evidence from the community care literature that the service will be narrowly defined and will not include the wide range of help and support that older people value so much – what have been called **low level preventative skills** like surveillance, befriending, companionship, financial tasks and practical tasks like changing bulbs, cleaning and unblocking sinks. It is these services, which have traditionally been the

province of the sheltered housing warden. Separating accommodation and care ensures that housing support services which researchers (Quilgars, 2000; Clark *et al*, 1998; Parkinson & Pierpoint, 2000) have shown to be critical to older people's wellbeing, will be delivered. The organisation that provides the accommodation will deliver associated housing services and the domiciliary care organisation will provide the care.

This argument in favour of the separation of housing support and care can, however, be reversed and used to argue for the delivery of a seamless service, one which avoids the demarcation of activities into care, support and housing management. Anchor schemes are examples of integrated accommodation and care, although the care its teams deliver is usually via a local authority contract. Anchor says it provides care in-house for two reasons. First, it wishes to avoid the problems, as it sees it, of fragmented management which separation of accommodation and care can bring. Second, it wants to be in control of the quality of care provided. It subscribes to a philosophy of care which is flexible, user-centred and based on principles of independent living. Anchor argues that some social services deliver services very differently and do not always subscribe to a philosophy of independent living. It does not want to work with social services which could '*insist on putting everybody to bed at 8.00 at night*'. Extra Care Charitable Trust (ECCT), another sizeable organisation in the very sheltered housing business, also firmly believes in the integration of housing management and care – in the principle, as the director called it, of a 'seamless service'. Housing management services and care services are completely fused. ECCT, somewhat ironically (it favours non-registered over registered provision), labels its approach '*the residential care approach*'. This it contrasts with the 'domiciliary approach', of which it is very critical. By the term '*a residential care approach*' it is referring to an holistic service.

> '*We offer a seamless service. We have staff on site who can deal with housing management issues as well as care issues. We feel this is important. For example, someone may be in rent arrears. Normally the daughter might pay the rent but hasn't been paying because her husband is terminally ill. We'd know this because of the integration of housing management with care. There might be a repair needed to a fixture that may have come off the wall. We might find that the fixture had come off the wall because the tenants had been using it for support so we could also assess the tenants' needs at the same time.*'
> (A scheme manager quoted in Woolham, 1998)

Abbeyfield houses illustrate a further aspect of the housing, support and care nexus. Abbeyfield has been operating very sheltered housing for a considerable length of time. The model operated separates the delivery of accommodation and care, but is different from those discussed thus far. Abbeyfield places a great deal of emphasis on what is now called low-level preventative support: a full meal service, cleaning, laundry, a resident housekeeper and more intangible benefits such as companionship. Personal care, where it is needed, is usually provided by social services or its agencies, although there are limited examples where some societies have decided to provide in-house care similar to the Anchor model. Where Abbeyfield differs from others is that its basic core service has been developed fully so that it includes activities which others may define as care. This core service edges up to but does not include the delivery of 'hands-on care'.

The above discussion illustrates the tensions which have bedevilled community care and supported housing for a considerable period of time which, despite its avowed intention, the *Supporting People* framework does not look like ending. Providers have continually been expected to separate out what is housing, what is support and what is care so that housing budgets do not pay for care, and social service budgets do not pay for the much more nebulous area of support. Providers have attempted to resist the rigid boundaries which governments want between housing, support and care because they know that their users' lives do not fragment along these lines. There has been no work to date on an older people's perspective on models of care and support in very sheltered housing. In the evaluation case study in **Chapter Five** we explore the consumer view. The key issue appears to be that very sheltered housing differs from residential care in that care is charged for separately and can be refused. Also, typically, the care is received on the basis of an individual social work assessment. These features apply in the Anchor or ECCT model described above (where care and accommodation form an integral service) as well as in the Hanover model. However, as the discussion on costs in the next chapter notes, some aspects of care are not necessarily charged for separately and the concept of a social service intermediary between user and the provider does not apply in the case of those who are not eligible for financial assistance.

Conclusions

This chapter has charted the main differences between schemes in terms of purpose, organisation and structure. All schemes claim to cater for ageing in place, but not all are committed to providing a 'home for life'. For some providers, a move to a nursing home or even a residential home does not signify failure. Schemes also differ in their approach to being an 'alternative to residential care'. This is a phrase which it is not easy to be precise about. It can mean accommodating the very same people who, in the absence of very sheltered housing, would have been admitted to residential care, or it can mean accommodating those who in the future might well become candidates for such care.

Most very sheltered housing is non-registered. The chapter has tried to tease out the pros and cons of registration. Registration is supposed to ensure protection for vulnerable people. But it is also by necessity inflexible; an overall fee is charged which covers accommodation, living costs and care. It may also be over-institutional in feel. There is no room for latitude and there is an unhelpful link between registration and the benefit system. By not being eligible for Housing Benefit and associated benefits, people may feel 'pauperised'. In theory, in non-registered provision, people can pick and choose much more what to have and what to spend, because the individual components of costs are separately charged for. The new *Care Standards Act* does not

seem to have resolved the anomaly of having two systems, registered and non-registered, each with different outcomes. Most very sheltered housing looks set to remain outside the *Act*'s jurisdiction, although the agency delivering the care service will probably be registered under it. However, the scheme itself will remain unregulated apart from self-enforcing codes of good practice such as that for supported housing developed by the National Housing Federation (Goss, 1998).

Finally, the chapter has looked at organisational structures. Service delivery can be 'separated' or 'integrated'. It is often supposed that, where accommodation and care are delivered by different organisations, registration will be 'avoided' and occupants will feel more empowered. However, a strong argument for the integration of accommodation, care and support is that the provider can be in full control of implementing its service philosophy and that a seamless or holistic service can be offered to tenants/residents. We know very little about what older people think are the virtues or otherwise of these different models.

Chapter Three
The new models: financial issues

It is in the area of costs that there has been the most evaluation, because a principal motivation behind development has been the belief that very sheltered housing may be a cheaper alternative to other forms of care. It is here that the greatest variation occurs. Three sets of published data were uncovered by this study:

- the Royal Commission's 'Six Vignettes' study (Royal Commission, 1999b)

- Hanover's comparison of the costs of private rented, Category 2 sheltered, extraCare housing (Hanover's term for very sheltered housing), registered residential care (Bartholomeou, 1999)

- the Cambridgeshire cost comparisons of residential care, very sheltered housing and domiciliary care (summarised in Fletcher *et al*, 1999).

In addition, there are a number of small, quite localised studies and, reported in Fletcher *et al* (1999), work in progress on cost effectiveness by Alex Marsh and Moyra Riseborough for Anchor Trust.

Throughout this discussion it is the costs of non-registered provision which are being considered and, where appropriate, compared with registered provision, ie residential care.

The main components of very sheltered housing costs

When comparisons are being made between very sheltered schemes, variation will be found in:

- gross rent levels

- rent/service charge ratios and the balance between eligible and ineligible items
- capital costs
- the way care services are provided for
- charging policies for care services.

Rents are subject to a great deal of variation due to regional location, whether the scheme is 'new build' or 'remodelled', the extent to which capital costs have been subsidised, and how, and whether or not revenue costs have been subsidised by Social Housing Management Grant. Tinker, in an earlier evaluation of very sheltered housing (1989), and in work carried out for the Royal Commission (1999b), found local authority very sheltered costs to be lower than housing association costs due to the way the warden costs in the former are shared throughout the whole stock and not directly met by very sheltered housing tenants. Very sheltered housing rents also vary according to their service charge component. It has already been suggested that very sheltered housing has developed opportunistically. The availability of Housing Benefit has been crucial, as has its role in funding what the Department of Social Security would now define as 'non-housing costs'. Oldman *et al* (1996) showed how supported and sheltered housing providers were able to use the Housing Benefit regulations to good effect. The Housing Benefit regulations have allowed the following service costs as eligible for Housing Benefit:

- cleaning of communal areas and cleaning of individual flats where the occupant is vulnerable

- alarm costs
- costs of equipment such as washing machines
- warden costs
- counselling and support costs.

Meals, heating, lighting, water and care costs are ineligible for Housing Benefit but Oldman *et al* (1996) and Cebulla *et al* (1999) have both shown the degree to which Housing Benefit has subsidised these costs. In the case of meals, heating and upkeep of communal areas, this has generally been with the connivance, albeit grudging, of Housing Benefit (HB) authorities. The *Supporting People* proposals were more concerned to end the well established practice of getting support costs paid for, overtly, by the social security system. The case of the treatment of meal charges in the HB regulations illustrates the subsidy point well. Where three meals are provided, seven days a week, as in Abbeyfield provision, the HB officer must follow the regulations and deduct only £18.65 a week (2000/2001 rates). The actual cost of meal provision is, however, higher.

The example below of one particular provider's rent breakdown for a one-bedroom very sheltered flat shows the service charge to be a significant proportion of the total rent and the element to be borne by the tenant – the ineligible charge – to be relatively low. This is one particular example. Oldman *et al* (1996) drew attention to the great variation in how different landlords structure rents, with some putting more rather than fewer costs within service charges and others putting similar costs into 'pure' rent.

In other examples provided for this study, the service charge element is a very much higher proportion of the gross rent and, arguably, until the recent tightening of existing HB regulations,

contained 'care' costs. Some very sheltered housing rents are very high and get close to residential care costs. It was argued in the last chapter that, residential care and very sheltered housing were distinct in that in the latter, housing, living costs and care were separately charged for. The reality is that this has not always been so. Sometimes an element of care costs have been 'wrapped up' in the rent.

The *Supporting People* implementation process will change rent structures greatly by taking out of the equation much of the service charge and putting it into the new local authority-administered *Supporting People* grant. At the time of writing, the Transitional Housing Benefit scheme is in operation. Very sheltered housing providers have a choice as to how much of current warden and other service costs to put into rent and how much to put into support (Schedule 1b in the Transitional Housing Benefit regulations). As one provider put it:

> 'We are playing a game of poker. If we put the lion's share into care rent we risk problems with local reference rents. If we put the lion's share into Schedule 1b we risk the possibility of the local authority refusing to pay up'.

Very little data was collected in this study on capital costs, but it appeared that reliance on Housing Corporation and other capital

Table 2.2	An example of a rent breakdown – 1998
Eligible rent	£105.85
Eligible service	£42.95
Total eligible	**£148.80**
Ineligible	
water rates	£1.47
heating	£2.35
lunch	£11.65
Total ineligible	**£15.47**

subsidies varied quite a bit. In some parts of the country, discussions are being held on the use of public and private finance initiatives for building very sheltered housing. But most providers in the study felt that the biggest obstacle to the continued development of very sheltered housing was the extreme dearth of capital subsidy.

The way care services are delivered and funded varies greatly. Tinker has suggested (Royal Commission, 1999b) that where services were internally delivered they were cheaper than those delivered by an external team. This conclusion may well be contested. Currently, a key feature of community care is the lack of consistency in local authority charging policies. In a decreasing number of local areas the care component is charged at zero cost to the user. Where the user is paying for care, one respondent in the study suggested that across the country the hourly rate for care varied within the range £3 to £15 an hour. In Lewisham's scheme cited by the Royal Commission (1999a, Ch. 10 Appendix) social services paid a flat-rate of £60 a week for each tenant, for whom the care was thus zero-priced. In some areas, charges are made even to those on Income Support, and some providers require users to give up a substantial share of their Attendance Allowance.

A key issue for tenants is the worry that care costs will increase as needs increase. The essence of Joseph Rowntree Housing Trust's continuing care community is that occupants have an option of paying a 'standard' community fee which covers all present and future needs.

Gross resource costs of very sheltered housing

The Royal Commission compared the national average cost of housing association very sheltered housing and ordinary sheltered housing. The figures in **Table 2.3**, below, were based on gross resource as opposed to cash costs, and exclude externally provided services. They are capital and running costs, relate to 1997/8 and are based on costings by Ernst & Young in *Living Independently* (McCafferty, 1994) and upratings in Netten and Dennett (1997).

Very sheltered housing compared with other provisions

The significance of the Royal Commission's use of resource costs is seen when comparisons are made between very sheltered housing and residential care, and between very sheltered housing and domiciliary care. Typically, in some studies, when comparisons are made, like is not being compared with like, and only accounting or cash costs are being presented, not economic or resource costs. Contentious claims have been made. Wolverhampton, for example, has argued that very sheltered housing costs approximately half the cost of residential care (Bailey, 1998). While it is true that social services do gain from a switch to very sheltered housing because their costs are being transferred to the DSS's budget, a resource-cost approach produces a different picture. The costing methodology proposed in the Royal Commission research report is recommended as a template for those undertaking cost comparisons. The costs figures produced by the two other studies looked at by this research, namely Bartholomeou and the

Table 2.3

Average gross resource costs of housing association and very sheltered housing

Very sheltered housing	£258.00	per week
Sheltered housing	£138.65	per week

Cambridgeshire study, did not include the costs of living at home.

> '*A like with like comparison of the cost of provision of services to someone living in an ordinary home with the cost of care in a very sheltered dwelling must include the cost of a home.*' (Royal Commission, 1999b)

The Royal Commission costings are also to be recommended because its assumptions are made absolutely explicit, even though they might not entirely be agreed with. For example, the very sheltered housing costings do not include the costs of adaptations, because it is assumed that such environments are barrier-free. Our own fieldwork suggests that this assumption cannot always be made. Nevertheless, the Commission's costings are very detailed and include components usually omitted by others, such as the costs of care management, the costs of adaptation, health care, respite care and housing costs, based on economic costings.

The Age Concern Institute of Gerontology (ACIOG) team make several points. First, comparison with residential care is difficult because of the big variation in the costs of the latter and difference in costs between local authority residential care and independent-sector homes. Second, very sheltered housing can bestow cost advantage because of economies of scale; night cover is cheaper than that provided in ordinary housing in the community and adaptations are not so necessary. Its conclusions, based on its vignette approach (hypothetical examples of people on the margins of residential care), are that, generally, very sheltered housing is not cheaper than care in an ordinary home. Whether residential care or ordinary housing is cheaper or more expensive than very sheltered housing depends on how many hours of home care, including night sitting,

are required and on how such care is provided by the staff of the very sheltered scheme. When only care costs are being compared, in four out of the five vignettes which included very sheltered housing it was cheaper than care delivered in ordinary housing.

The figures in **Table 2.4**, opposite, illustrate the point that generalisations cannot be made about comparisons. The table focuses on the Royal Commission research's *Vignettes One* and *Three*. They depend on particular circumstances. In both vignettes, very sheltered housing is ranked third in order of expense, but in *Vignette One* very sheltered housing is a little more expensive than care in ordinary housing, and in *Vignette Three* very sheltered housing is a lot cheaper. The explanation for this discrepancy is that, in the second example, large amounts of home care are needed which in the very sheltered or residential care setting can be provided by staff who do not need to be in a one-to-one ratio. *Vignette One* depicts a man aged 65–74 and living with a spouse. He is often awake and active at night. During the day he uses the toilet frequently and needs some help and supervision. His wife has arthritis and finds it difficult to get up the stairs. The woman in *Vignette Three* is a highly dependent woman, a wheelchair user, living alone, with no cognitive impairment.

The Royal Commission also examined where costs fell. It concluded that at modest income levels disposable income was very much the same under each care package. However, this is not so for public agencies. The analysis shows how the vagaries of the current funding system favour very sheltered housing because the DSS is bearing a significant element of costings. *Supporting People* will have a profound effect on comparative costings. So too might the implementation of the *Care Standard Act*, which will have an impact on the costs of registered provision.

Table 2.4	Comparisons of total costs of different environments per annum	
	Vignette One	*Vignette Three*
In own home		
ordinary housing	£17, 253.00	£41,740.00
very sheltered housing	£18,188.00	£37,322.00
Full-time residential care		
local authority	£21,399.00	£21,285.00
private	£16,646.00	£16,532.00

Note: The costs used here are resource costs and include the following: home environment, day and night care, personal household care, health care, respite care, counselling, care management housing and income support.

So it has been shown that very sheltered housing is not usually cheaper than care at home and is usually more expensive than residential care. The other studies which were looked at came to different conclusions but employed different methodologies. *Table 2.5*, below, shows Bartholomeou's conclusions.

The approach adopted was to take one hypothetical case and place that person who is in receipt of ten hours of care in different settings. In terms of cost to the public purse, Bartholomeou ranks as follows in order of expense: private rented, Category 2 sheltered housing, very sheltered housing and residential care. The Cambridgeshire study (Fletcher *et al*, 1999) comes to different conclusions about cost to the public purse and argues that the overall cost of very sheltered housing to the public purse is slightly lower than for residential care. It is not easy to see all the assumptions that have been made by these two studies, and they have not employed resource costs.

Cost to the user

Most studies, including the Royal Commission's, pay insufficient attention to further factors which have a bearing on costs, namely the contribution of informal carers and affordability. The first point is taken up in **Chapter Five** – the contribution of the relative to very sheltered housing seems to affect total costs. Where the relative is maintaining their role as informal carer, costs both to the public purse and to the individual tenant come down. On the second point the Royal Commission concludes that for people on modest incomes disposable incomes are comparable whatever the care package. The data available to this study challenges this point. Bartholomeou (1999) also comes to a different conclusion from that of the Royal Commission. She argues that residential care significantly pauperises its occupants and concludes that the same person (entitled to financial help from the state) has £152.23

Table 2.5	Very sheltered housing compared with other provisions			
	Private rented	Cat. 2 sheltered housing	Very sheltered housing	Residential care
Total housing and support costs (includes board and care costs)	£140.70	£70.34	£158.03	£262.70

in 'disposable income' after housing and support costs have been paid when living in very sheltered housing. In making comparisons between living in very sheltered housing and residential care, assumptions have to be very robust. The gap between the two disposable incomes will be a function of the level of care and its cost to the sheltered tenant and how much is spent on food, heat, lighting, water, etc, as well as on the degree of Housing Benefit subsidy going into this scheme.

We appear to know very little about older people's own views on the disposable income/pauperisation issue, although there is in Fletcher *et al* (1999) reference to a scheme in Wolverhampton which changed its status from registered to de-registered. Occupants' pocket money apparently increased from £14.50 (as it was then) to £100 a week. They reported that they had more choice and freedom to go out and spend money on presents and so on.

It will be clear by now what an enormous contribution Housing Benefit has made to the financial viability and hence affordability of schemes. The Survey of English Housing 1998/1999 shows that 75% of sheltered housing tenants receive Housing Benefit.

There must be some concern about the affordability of very sheltered housing to that minority of older tenants who will get no help with either their housing or care costs apart from receiving, if eligible, the non-means-tested Attendance Allowance. It has been shown that very sheltered housing rents can be very high. For that group of ex-owner occupiers who are 'not rich, not poor' there is something of a perverse incentive to enter residential care. The means test used results in people getting public support at higher levels of income than those operating for deciding eligibility for Housing Benefit.

Table 2.6, below, shows an example from data collected in the course of this study. It illustrates some of the issues which have come up in this chapter. It roughly supports Bartholomeou's conclusions, above. The figures relate to a couple who are both on the margins of residential care. A couple have been chosen for this example because, as **Chapter Five** suggests, very sheltered housing is 'good' for couples and residential care 'bad'. They were typical of most very sheltered housing tenants in that they were receiving benefits, but they were not typical in that their benefit income was very high. Both received the double rate of Attendance

Table 2.6	The costs of living in a very sheltered housing scheme		
Income per week		**Expenditure per week**	
State pension	£107.65	Rent and service charge	£15.00
Occupational pensions	£46.67	Fuel	£10.00
Income from investments	–	Meals	£35.00
Income from benefits		Other food	£40.00
Housing Benefit	£51.00	Personal care/general assistance – 13 hrs per week	£31.80
		Other eg telephone, hair, chiropody	£14.00
Attendance Allowance	£107.10		
Total (excluding Housing Benefit)	**£261.42**	**Total**	**£145.80**

Allowance; this is hard to get and there might be an issue with some benefit offices about receiving it in sheltered housing. Their care is relatively cheap compared with many other examples obtained during this study, and so is the rent.

Their disposable income is shown to be, after essential costs have been paid, well over £100. Residential care in the area covered in this example was £230 for local-authority-funded clients. Here, their only income would be £15.45 a week. However, all costs, except for those designated as 'other' in the table, would be covered. They would not, as clients funded by a local authority, be eligible for Attendance Allowance.

Conclusions

Schemes vary considerably in how their costs are structured. A resource approach to costing shows that very sheltered housing is rarely cheaper than domiciliary care and is usually more expensive than residential care. The social security input often makes very sheltered housing the most expensive option in terms of costs to the public purse. However, where cash costs are the focus, conclusions are different, and very sheltered housing is shown to be a very favourable option due to economies of scale and the role of Housing Benefit. Very sheltered housing is made affordable by Housing Benefit. For those who formerly owned their own homes and who are neither rich nor poor, there must be some worry about affordability. However, we still know little about the relationship between costs and quality.

Chapter Four

Moving into and living in the new models

Moving into very sheltered housing

The social care literature suggests that most older people move fairly reluctantly into residential care. In the first instance, at least, others put forward the idea of the move. We know less about moves to housing-based models of provision. England *et al* (2000) has noted that relatives, GPs and others play a key role in the decision to move to sheltered housing and, initially at least, the older person may be reluctant. However, whether or not the move to very sheltered housing is one which has clearly been decided upon by the older person themselves, it is subject to an assessment process. Very sheltered housing is, in the main, located in the social rented sector, is a scarce resource and is thus accessed through the rules of welfare allocation.

The desire to opt positively for collective living in later life is not unknown in Britain, although rarer than in Europe or the USA. Brenton (1998) has examined the Dutch co-housing model, whereby older people opt to live together, giving each other social and mutual support. There are around 200 such groups in the Netherlands where people have made an unfettered decision to live in age-segregated environments.

One Dutch co-housing resident is reported to have said:

'....it's important to move while you still can to a place you choose before other people move you to a place they choose' (Armstrong, 1993, quoted in Brenton, 1998).

It was noted in **Chapter One** that the social climate in Britain has not been a propitious one for collective living arrangements, particularly in later life. Moving to age-segregated environments is seen by policy makers as alien to the idea of independent living in ordinary surroundings in the 'community'. However, some older people in Britain do make such choices. Research on the private retirement housing sector (Oldman, 1991) suggests that it could not have developed if the idea of living with people of a similar age had been an entirely unattractive concept. Hartrigg Oaks near York explicitly appeals to those people who want to join a community of a similar generation and of similar interests. Although it by no means sought them out, the Joseph Rowntree Housing Trust marketed its village concept to Quaker communities around Britain. Although the Dutch co-housing model, where a group gets together and plans the whole project from acquisition of land through to moving in, is almost non-existent in Britain, living together in later life does appeal to some older people in this country.

The opportunity afforded by increasing levels of housing equity

There is a growing group of older people for whom moving positively to an age-segregated environment could be a reality. It is now very well known that there is a substantial cohort of older home owners with not insignificant levels of housing wealth. However, they have had little opportunity to employ that equity for purposes of accessing supportive environments. Residential care in Britain is unpopular; it is only available on a weekly charge basis and houses have often to be sold, and housing wealth exhausted to pay for it. With a few notable exceptions,[1] very sheltered housing has been unavailable in the private sector and owner occupiers' wealth may bar them from entering schemes in the social rented sector. There is evidence that the retirement housing industry is poised to move into very sheltered housing.

Levels of housing wealth vary considerably and many owner occupiers would not be able to purchase very sheltered housing outright. The circumstances of the 'not rich, not poor' older owner occupier are gradually being recognised by developers. Subsidised leasehold schemes such as those managed by Anchor Trust's subsidiary, Guardian, have been around for some years, but like private-sector retirement housing have been very limited in what they offer in terms of support services. Now, however, both Laing and Buisson (1998) and the Elderly Accommodation Counsel[2] report a number of shared owner-ship assisted-living schemes either in the

pipeline or in management. One such example is the ExtraCare Charitable Trust scheme in Wellingborough.

A further development in the private sector is the emergence of a private rented very sheltered market. Laing and Buisson has commented:

'Until recently the capital requirements of new private sector retirement housing for letting might have restricted the growth of that market, but the rapid expansion of sale and leaseback and other forms of securitisation for care homes suggests that capital may be readily available to develop privately rented housing' (1998).

Rent levels are likely to be very high; in the example (see footnote, below) rents are £450 a week.[3]

There are a limited number of mixed-tenure schemes, the best known of which is ECCT's retirement village, Berryhill. Older people are offered the opportunity either to rent or to buy.

As with moves to residential care, older people who are in a position to self-fund are not always able to exercise choice fully. Allocation criteria may be in operation; for example for-purchase schemes may be reluctant to take people with dementia, regardless of their financial circumstances. However, even in schemes which have a majority of self-funders, allocation criteria can be in operation. For example, applicants to Hartrigg Oaks have to meet certain health criteria and are asked to complete a questionnaire. The model is based on actuarial principles; its financial viability is threatened if care needs are too heavy.

---

[1] One such being Retirement Security Limited, a company which in the 1980s and 1990s developed private-sector very sheltered housing and very ingeniously utilised the Income Support system to assist owner occupiers with ongoing costs.

[2] Personal correspondence with the Director.

[3] Known to the author as Sunrise Private Rented Assisted Living.

Black and minority ethnic older people

Just as ex-owner occupiers are less likely than those who used to rent to move into very sheltered housing in the social sector, most schemes are predominantly white. Until recently there has been little interest in very sheltered housing provision for black and minority ethnic older people. However, there is evidence that this is changing a little. A dedicated scheme, not dissimilar to Hartrigg Oaks (in the main, for white, middle-class older people), may be a positive alternative to residential care or living with families for the fast-growing ethnic elder population. Fletcher *et al* (1999) detailed such a scheme for the West Indian community in Nottingham.

Assessment criteria

In the study, the models varied in terms of how assessment procedures for governing access to very sheltered housing worked and who was involved in carrying them out. The last chapter has suggested that schemes' aims differed. They fell into two broad groups: those that can be categorised as re-inventions of residential care and those that can be categorised as remodelled sheltered housing. Allocation criteria reflected these different aims. Where the explicit aim was to divert from residential care, social services tended to be centrally involved and, in some cases, were selecting tenants from the residential care list. More typically, social services shared the assessment task with others. Allocation panels, comprising representatives from social services, the housing department and the provider, were fairly common. Social services may have a percentage of nominations to a scheme, and assessment procedures may be similar to care management processes which are used generally to allocate social care. Seymour's (1997)

evaluation of the London Borough of Lewisham's first very sheltered housing illustrates the difficulties involved in defining what diversion from residential care means and in devising procedures that are transparent, understood and 'owned' by all involved. The scheme is described as being targeted at '*particularly frail and vulnerable people as a direct alternative to residential care*', but this target group is defined as '*frail older people who are finding it difficult living and caring for themselves in their own homes but are independent enough **not** [author's emphasis] to be offered residential care*'. In the end, further allocation objectives were added:

- the provision of a cost effective alternative for people living at home and receiving a very high-cost package

- the provision of housing with the security of 24-hour care for frail elderly people who feel vulnerable and are afraid of living alone in the community

- the provision of a preventative service which will enable vulnerable people who might in the future have entered residential care to remain in the community and retain their independence

- the decision that the service is not appropriate for people who are likely to deteriorate rapidly.

Not surprisingly, there was disagreement as to who would benefit from very sheltered housing. Some providers argued for 'balance' in their allocation criteria. Maintaining a mix of dependency levels does not upset staffing levels and helps achieve a vibrant community where a good quality of life is as important as the quality of care. Moreover, tenancies should be offered at the right moment, before health deteriorates. But others felt that very sheltered housing was a scarce resource and so all tenancies should be allocated to people with relatively high needs. Some of the providers in the study, however, employed allocation criteria that were akin to those used for ordinary sheltered housing. Housing need played a more prominent role. A further approach was to allocate tenancies to 'younger' people for whom other provisions were considered inappropriate; examples given were people with mental health problems or who had a history of self-neglect.

Some providers operated exclusion criteria, for example not offering tenancies to those with dementia or a history of aggressive or abusive behaviour. Others accepted those whose dementia was at an early stage or offered a double tenancy to people with dementia who had a spouse who had been the principal carer.

Moving in: the physical environment

Hanover has contributed to a debate about the physical aspects of very sheltered housing through the publication of a design manual (Robson *et al*, 1997). The key physical difference between residential care and very sheltered housing lies in living space. Typically, a very sheltered housing flat will be around 45 square metres while a room in a residential home is likely to be something in the region of 10–12 square metres. Schemes varied in other ways: in number of units, whether they were purpose-built or adapted, the extent to which they were accessible environments, and in *living space:communal space* ratios. At one end of the continuum, in terms of size, in the models covered by this study, were JRHT and ECCT's retirement villages with around 200 residents; at the other end was Abbeyfield's shared housing with 6–8 residents. Commissioners and providers had different views about the optimum size of a scheme; these views were based on the perceived benefits of economies of scale rather than on any view of what older people themselves feel. Some felt that

schemes with over 40 units were in danger of looking institutional, but that a reasonable size was needed to accommodate a wide range of needs. A number of providers were beginning to think about design features for people with memory problems, such as colour-coding, landmarking and signing.

Anchor and Hanover had rather different views on *communal:private space* ratios. The former tries to keep communal facilities to a minimum in order to achieve a domestic and non-institutional feel. Hanover, by contrast, places some importance on the provision of shops, attractive lounges, hairdressing salons and so on. The schemes in the study with the highest level of facility – including jacuzzi, fitness centre, library, IT suite and arts and crafts areas – were Hartrigg Oaks and Berryhill. The motive was similar – to provide a lively and interesting environment.

The role of assistive technology remains largely unexplored in the context of service provision for older people. Alarms, one of the most established types, have been an essential feature of sheltered housing since its inception. However, less is known about the usefulness in the sheltered housing context of some other applications, such as mobility aids, aids to daily living, environ-mental control systems and surveillance systems. Very sheltered housing should be a barrier-free environment, but a number of commentators suggested that this was not always achieved.

The whole area of physical design in very sheltered housing is one which remains largely unresearched. It is not known what older people, both current and prospective occupants, feel about different styles or what contributes to a scheme looking, and hence feeling, institutional. It may be that the notion of 'your own front door' is a hollow one if that front door looks out onto a long and unattractive corridor.

Services and service delivery

All the providers in the study claimed that service delivery was underpinned by a commitment to the principles of independent living which marked out their provision from that commonly available in residential care. It was argued that the concept of 'your own front door' and the reality of a housing environment favour and allow the delivery of independent living principles. Twigg (1997) contends that care deliverers behave differently according to the setting. An older person's home cannot be under the control of professionals, and the norms of privacy, autonomy and identity embodied in the concept of home are shared by service providers and applied in other people's homes as well as their own. However, there is a counter-argument (Baldwin *et al*, 1993; Reed & Payton, 1996; Gavilan, 1992) that suggests that institutionalisation of frail older people is endemic, whatever the setting. Ill-health and immobility institutionalise older people and the process of assessment and subsequent care delivery from bureaucratic organisations exacerbates an older person's dependent status wherever they are living.

Most of the schemes in the study were accommodating a range of disability levels. At least some of the residents/tenants were highly dependent and resembled the case studies in the Royal Commission's six vignette studies. The three types of need classified by Davies *et al* (1990) – long-interval, short-interval and critical-interval[4] – appeared to be represented. All the schemes provided the following help to at least some of their residents:

- preparing meals and eating

- dressing and undressing
- getting in and out of bed
- washing, bathing and use of toilet in addition to help with domestic and other practical support like shopping and collecting prescriptions.

The number of total 'care' hours going into a scheme varied; for example, in two 30-unit schemes one had 180 hours and the other 300. The definition of the word 'care' proved problematic. Typically, it included domestic help as well as personal care, but some providers used the word only to refer to the rather narrow formulation which has become a feature of British community care. Some providers were able to give quite detailed information on care hours. Some providers, Anchor being an example, had managed to secure a number of hours over and above those allocated to individual tenants, for social and related activities. In Hanover's case Bartholomeou (1999) reported that the average number of care hours received is 9 hours, the highest being 22 hours a week. (In another scheme in the study the highest number of hours received by an individual tenant was 30 hours.)

Typically, when people moved into a scheme, an assessment was carried out of their care needs, a care plan drawn up and a keyworker allocated. There was no evidence that that process was controlled by the user – but we return to that point in the next chapter. However, respondents said that they tried to promote independence – encouraged residents to do things for themselves and were strongly committed to a process of rehabilitation. Some stressed the flexibility of their service; for example, the amount of care received might be increased after an

---

[4] *Long-interval needs:* unable to perform one or more domestic tasks which need to be undertaken occasionally but less often than daily; *short-interval:* unable to perform one or more domestic tasks which need to be undertaken frequently (that is, more than daily); *critical-interval:* unable to perform crucial self-care tasks which need to be undertaken frequently and at short notice.

illness or after a period in hospital but reduced again when more independence was regained.

With two exceptions, providers seemed unclear about the contribution of relatives to the total amount of care and support provided. Our conclusion is that what most marks out very sheltered housing from residential care is the contribution of relatives. Seymour (1997), in her evaluation of Lewisham's scheme, comments:

> *'This* [relatives' support] *is one of the value-added aspects of a very sheltered scheme which would be unlikely to occur in residential care'.*

Seymour also notes that very sheltered housing may differ significantly from residential care in the degree of mutual support that goes on.

The way service delivery is organised differed. **Chapter Two** distinguished two broad types of scheme: those where accommodation and care were provided by different organisations and those where they are provided by the same organisation. Within these two broad groupings there were differences. For example, in most ECCT schemes accommodation and care are, strictly speaking, delivered by different organisations with, typically, a registered housing association owning the property and ECCT providing management services. However, these cover accommodation-related activities, such as what is called, in supported housing, 'intensive housing management', as well as care and support services. A key issue for all schemes is the achievement of that chimera, the 'seamless service'. This can be difficult where accommodation and care are unambiguously separated, as in Hanover schemes.

For some years there has been relentless debate within the sheltered housing sector about the role of the warden (see particularly Hasler & Page, 1998). As far as very sheltered housing is concerned, the debate has still some way to go. In some schemes the role has disappeared, and been replaced by a scheme manager who manages the total service: housing, care and support. In others the post remains, although renamed 'estate manager'. With the advent of *Supporting People*, the funding, and hence the role of the warden, has become uncertain, but research suggests that the low-level, preventative, housing support activities provided by the warden are highly valued by tenants and relatives (England *et al*, 2000).

Typically, but not invariably, schemes had their own dedicated team of care workers who sometimes were deliberately not called such but rather 'support workers' or some other such term. Some teams undertook everything, including tenants' cleaning. Other schemes had a separate domestic team. There was no evidence that staff had received any bespoke training which might focus on the independent living principles which are intended to be the hallmark of very sheltered housing.

Night cover was a contentious issue. Although it is sometimes regarded as one of the defining features of very sheltered housing, by no means everyone subscribed to this view. Some providers deliberately did not offer 24-hour cover (other than through a dispersed alarm service), sometimes to avoid registration and sometimes because they believed that to do so would threaten the enabling, non-institutional ethos of their scheme. Where on-site night cover was provided, it was usually but not always 'sleeping' cover. It could always be bought in on a temporary basis for specific tenants when the need arose. Some providers, however, claimed that if a scheme was claiming to provide a home for life, catering for needs as they progressed, night cover was essential.

The issue of dementia absorbed providers in the study. All sheltered housing schemes will accommodate some sufferers; Bartholomeou (1999) has estimated that 13% of Hanover's extraCare residents have dementia. Kitwood *et al* (1995) suggested that, with care and training, sheltered housing can relatively comfortably accommodate the problem. In our study, providers generally felt that severe dementia could threaten the sense of community they strove to create. Some were giving a great deal of thought to providing special wings or schemes for people with dementia. In the past it has been assumed that provision for people with dementia will always be located within residential home settings because of the risks involved and the levels of care delivered. More recently it is argued that small, domestic, housing-based settings are more appropriate, partly because relatives can more easily stay involved. There are now a number of interesting such examples around the country and examples provided by the Royal Commission (1999b Ch. 10 Appendix E).

Schemes provided or encouraged social activities. Some providers felt that they would prefer them to be organised by the tenants themselves and that too much emphasis on organised social life could upset the non-institutional feel of a scheme. All schemes provided a dining room and the provision of at least one meal a day; however, only one provider, Hanover, made this a condition of the tenancy.

Most of the schemes had residents' meeting but there was little evidence of residents' committees with real influence.

Conclusions

In the last chapter, in the discussion on costs, it was suggested that very sheltered housing can be more expensive than both residential and domiciliary care. Issues of quality were ignored. What we really do not know very much about is the interaction of care, quality and costs. We do not know much about the adequacy of care and support in the different variants of very sheltered housing nor how adequacy of care and support compares in different settings – in very sheltered housing, in residential care and at home. Much previous research has focused on quantitative issues such as hours delivered. We do not, however, know much about:

- whether the care and support feel different from those received elsewhere

- whether the care provided is enough, too much or what is wanted

- whether care is less important in a non-disabling environment that allows people to do much more for themselves and what difference the provision of at least one meal a day makes

- whether care is less important in an environment where people feel much more positive about themselves than they did in the past

- whether the relationship between relative and tenant has changed and the move to very sheltered housing makes it easier for the relative to go on caring.

Chapter Five looks at these difficult issues.

Chapter Five

Evaluating very sheltered housing

There has been no recent comprehensive evaluation of the new forms of provision. In particular, no real attempt has been made to assess outcomes and/or the quality of care being delivered. Tinker's (1989) national study, covering both local authority and housing association schemes, is now out of date. The Department of Environment's study *Living Independently* (McCafferty, 1994) included very sheltered housing in its coverage but cannot really be regarded as being evaluative in its scope. Its remit was different. It was to provide a sound basis for making resource decisions concerning housing provision for older and disabled people. Fletcher *et al*'s study (1999) of very sheltered housing has already been drawn upon. It focuses on the strategic issues involved in commissioning very sheltered housing and sets out good practice in this area. Since the Tinker and *Living Independently* studies there have been a small number of evaluative studies of very sheltered housing, most of which have been referred to above. One which has not is of particular interest to this chapter. It is research by the University of Keele comparing the residents of Broadway Gardens, Wolverhampton Borough Council's first very sheltered scheme, with older people living in ordinary housing. The researchers concluded that the Broadway Gardens group had better health outcomes (Royal Commission, 1999b Ch. 10 Annex E).

It became very clear in the course of this study that evaluation of the newer forms of provision is problematic, partly because aims are unclear and hence difficult to measure. Moreover, since by their very nature they are neither properly 'housing provision' nor properly 'care provision', 'off-the-shelf' methodologies such as those which have been used to measure the quality of care in residential settings are inappropriate. Sheltered housing, by contrast, has never been the subject of sophisticated evaluation. The central problem for any evaluation of service provision is finding a way of assessing outcomes. It is not so difficult to obtain measures which are input- and output-based, but much harder to focus on the impact of service provision. Baldock has noted:

> 'There are many ways of measuring the benefits of interventions, all of them imperfect; do they prevent entry into residential care, do they affect the expressed satisfaction of users and carers, do they reduce the chance of falling and other accidents and problems, do they affect measures of depression and anxiety, do they slow the increase in disabilities, and, ultimately, do they extend life?' (Baldock, 1997).

The purpose of this chapter is to present a 'pilot' evaluation of York's two initiatives. These are first described and then the methodology used is presented.

A description of the York schemes

The first of these was developed by Joseph Rowntree Housing Trust (JRHT) and the second by the City of York Council, significantly a unitary authority with a community services department which merged the housing and social services departments. It has a strong purchaser–provider split.

Red Lodge

JRHT established its initiative, 'flexi-care', in Red Lodge, a large Category 2 sheltered housing scheme in New Earswick, near York. In 1992, just before the changes in the funding of residential care, it registered up to 13 of its sheltered units as residential care places under the *Registered Homes Act*. The number of units could vary and any one residential unit could fluctuate with demand. Its purpose was to avoid the trauma of moving to residential care. The older person could stay in the same flat they had always lived in, but change from being a tenant to a being a resident. The initiative has evolved. At present there are 32 registered units, and this is likely to increase shortly to 42 units. The registered units are no longer dispersed around the scheme, but almost all are located in one wing. The majority of the residential units used to be sheltered housing and hence are much larger than most residential care rooms, and have kitchens, living room and bedroom(s). The scheme has generous communal facilities and a day centre which is used by older people living nearby. Two meals a day can be purchased. In terms, then, of the classification system used in this report, Red Lodge is both registered and non-registered. It accommodates residents and tenants. The former pay an inclusive fee for all services: accommodation, living costs and care. The latter pay separately for these different components. Those people who transfer from the sheltered side of the scheme to the residential side change, therefore, their financial status.

Red Lodge accommodates people with a wide range of needs, and the accommodation, care and support are operated by the same organisation. On this latter point Red Lodge is a complicated care 'marketplace'. On the residential side, half of the residents are self-funding and the others funded through local authority contracts. On the sheltered housing side, it has nine tenants who are receiving care packages delivered by the same in-house team that looks after people in the residential units. There are also some tenants who receive support from agencies contacted to provide home care from York Social Services. Finally, a few people make their own arrangements and buy private domestic help or care. At the time of the fieldwork, 23 units were registered. The scheme is managed by a head of home and includes among its complement of staff a warden who provides a service to the sheltered tenants.

Glen Lodge and Barstow House

The City of York initiative consists of two supported housing schemes (not officially designated 'sheltered' housing or 'very sheltered' housing), Glen Lodge and Barstow House, each with about 30 units. They were formerly Part III homes (local authority residential care) with sheltered housing bungalows attached. In 1998/9 they were refurbished for around £1m each of 'housing money'. They mostly comprise one-bedroom self-contained flats with showers, not baths. They have assisted bathing facilities and, like Red Lodge, generous communal facilities. One meal a day can be purchased. Although not explicitly declared, the general purpose of the schemes is to 'divert people from residential care'. Accommodation, care and support are provided by one organisation, the City of York Council. The 'scheme manager' (not warden) manages a team of ten on-site 'support workers' (not carers) who provide the full range of personal care and domestic support to those who need or want it. Night cover (sleeping or waking) is not available but, as in any other sheltered housing scheme, tenants can get through to York's central control and a mobile warden will attend to the emergency.

Comparison

The two initiatives are sufficiently different from each other to provide opportunity for useful comparison, and many of the issues raised thus far in the report can be explored with older people. What it is not possible to do is to undertake a comparison between schemes where accommodation, care and support are integrated with those where the three are delivered by different organisations. Both initiatives were examples of integrated provision.

The evaluative approach adopted

The starting point was that the evaluation should have a strong user perspective. Previous tenant satisfaction surveys have tended to assume, not probe for, the benefits of living in very sheltered housing. Yet it is relatively new and there is very little of it. The focus group research carried out for the Royal Commission by the ACIOG team (Royal Commission, 1999b) suggested that older people are uncertain what is meant by sheltered housing and were confused as to the difference between it and residential care.

The approach that was adopted was qualitative. We wanted to let tenants 'speak

for themselves' (Gubrium, 1993). The aim was to listen to their accounts of why they had moved and to find out whether their expectations had matched their experience. There is an extensive literature on evaluation of residential care. Methodologies do not necessarily travel well to other contexts and there has been a tendency in residential care research to measure quality 'top down' rather than explore in great depth what is salient to older people. For example, there has been some work trying to measure whether the Department of Health's six basic values listed in *Homes are for Living In* (privacy, dignity, independence, choice, rights and fulfilment) get implemented. However, research such as that conducted by Raynes (1999) and Oldman and Quilgars (1999) suggests that issues to do with the standards of care provision are less important to residents than things like having enough to do, having people to talk to, living in a pleasant environment and so on.

The interviews with providers and other key players in the study had suggested there were some key questions which could inform the design of the fieldwork.

- What does the concept 'your own front door' mean?

- Is 'independent living' being achieved?

- What contribution do relatives make to life in very sheltered housing?

- How affordable is very sheltered housing?

On the first point above we attempted to explore what sort of place people felt they were living in. Higgins's (1989) framework (referred to at the beginning of **Chapter One**) was used to locate the initiatives on an institution/home continuum. Do people feel it is like living 'in a home' or 'at home'?

---

[1] Sixteen interviews and one focus group were held with the City of York tenants and twenty interviews were held with both tenants and residents living in JRHT's Red Lodge. The latter fieldwork was mainly conducted a year earlier than that in the City of York schemes.

So the starting point were semi-structured interviews with a total of 36 tenants/residents[1] (for an example of topic guides used see **Appendix B**). Interviews with relatives were also an important key feature of the fieldwork; two focus groups were conducted comprising a total of 16 relatives of tenants in both Glen Lodge and Barstow House. In addition, the fieldwork compared views on the initiatives held by the different interested parties: older people managers, staff, care purchasers and care regulators. The topic guides used mirrored that used for tenants.

As well as establishing whether older people and providers share the same concept of very sheltered housing, the aim of this 'stakeholder' approach was to explore whether the schemes' avowed objectives were being met. This last task was problematic in that, like so many other providers, both case study providers had not got clearly articulated objectives. The City of York appeared to be committed to the principle of diverting from residential care, maximising independence and improving people's quality of life. JRHT wanted to avoid people having to undertake a traumatic move to a more intensive form of provision.

Moving in

It was difficult to establish whether the City of York schemes were diverting from residential care, without attempting to be very precise about what that phrase means. Certainly some people required a great deal of help, and without Glen Lodge or Barstow House might well have gone into a home. However, these people only represented around a third of the tenant population. Another third were designated 'medium' dependent – that is, they needed help with domestic tasks and with the occasional personal care task. The final third were similar in characteristics to ordinary sheltered housing populations. Even the 'top third' were diverse. For example, one woman was simply very old, 92 years. She had moved from an ordinary sheltered housing scheme; she said of herself '*I was really a bit feeble*'. Four or five others had had very serious operations and could not have coped at home. However, had there been excellent rehabilitative facilities in York the move to the schemes might not have been so necessary. The remaining members of the high-dependency group were declining physically and finding coping difficult. Two were at pains to stress that they had been very dependent on relatives looking after them in their own home and that the move represented greater independence. Three of the relatively independent group had had spouses who either had had dementia or had been very physically dependent. Their moves had been based principally on the extent of their spouse's needs. One man in the relatively independent group had been desperately lonely and depressed living by himself.

There had been some reluctance about moving into the scheme, with the exception of one woman of 64 who had planned the whole thing herself.

> '*I came in anticipation. I will be in a wheelchair all the time soon, I'm told. I wanted to pick where I wanted to go now.*'

For the majority, however, it was clear from both the tenant and relative interviews that relatives had been a major influence in suggesting the move to very sheltered housing. There were worries that the move would be unpleasant and would threaten independence.

As far as Red Lodge was concerned, two sets of 'moving in' had to be explored. The first related to why the sheltered housing tenants had moved in originally, and the second to why the residents had moved into the care side. The sheltered tenants had moved in primarily for 'housing' reasons and had aged 'in place'. Only eight of the residents on the registered side of the scheme had moved from the sheltered side, the rest having moved from outside the scheme. Generally, all were resigned to the move. However, those who had previously been Red Lodge tenants were very pleased not to have had to move to a different residential home. One woman with visual impairment was delighted that she did not have to 'learn' new surroundings. Those who had moved from outside were highly satisfied with their living space, which they knew was more generous than in most other residential care. Residents were not always clear why the move had happened. Three people had been very worried about what they considered would be a reduction in their living standards. The decision about whether to move to the residential side of the scheme was a hard one. The following comment from a Red Lodge tenant was in favour:

> 'We want to plan our own lives. We don't want our family to do what we had to do when my mother refused to go into nursing care'.

This comment from another tenant was against:

> 'They take all your money and I'm frightened I will lose my privacy. The night staff come in and I won't know'.

At the time of writing, the City of York Registration and Inspection Unit was having an influence on the decision to move from the sheltered to the residential side of Red Lodge. The argument was put that JRHT was providing all three components of registered care: accommodation, board and personal care to sheltered tenants. Accordingly, it required those people on care packages to convert to residential status. Not everyone involved could be described as being on the margins of residential care. One woman, for example, simply bought herself meals and paid for two assisted baths a week from the in-house team.

Living in a home or living at home

At the beginning of this report Higgins' (1989) institution/home dichotomy was discussed. For the very sheltered housing tenants interviewed in this study, their living circumstances had the attributes of home not institution.

The majority of the City of York tenants felt that what they were living in was their own home, although the experience was very different from living in their previous house. But it was strongly contrasted to living in a home. In common with most older people, they did not relish the prospect of going into a residential home.

> 'I shouldn't have liked a home. I like to run my own life, I'm afraid.'

> 'I would be upset going into residential care but I can't do a lot.'

The words the City of York tenants used for describing where they were living varied but almost always they implied independent living.

> 'It's not a home, we are all in flats.'

> 'I call it supported housing.'

> 'One thing I don't call it. I don't call it an old people's home. I look after myself.'

> 'I just call it Glen Lodge flatlets.'

Tenants said they had problems explaining to others what their living circumstances were, and they did not like the fact that it was often assumed they were in a home.

*'Everyone presumes it is a nursing home:
"What did you want to go there for?",
I frequently get asked. I really resent
the question.'*

GPs were reported to misunderstand the
purpose of the schemes; they would ask the
manager about a tenant instead of going
directly to that tenant's flat.

But three tenants did feel that what they
were living in was more of an institution than
a home. One person said:

'It's residential, isn't it?'

All the relatives felt very clear that the
initiatives were not residential care.

*'You get as much or as little care
as you like.'*

Housing managers and operational staff had
a different perspective from each other.
The former thought that the schemes could
replace residential care for many people but
the latter felt that, although the provision
could, over time, edge right up to residential
care, it was quite distinct from it. People had
to be able to look after themselves fairly well.
Social services staff were the most sceptical
about the initiative's ability to divert from
residential care.

The two City of York schemes were new.
The older of the two, Glen Lodge, had only
been open 18 months. It was not possible in
the timescale of the research to measure
whether the schemes were being successful
at providing a 'home for life'. During that time
there had been a 14% turnover, attributable
to deaths, or moves to nursing or residential
care. The issue of whether the schemes were
homes for life was a difficult one for people.
Tenants and relatives alike suspected that
when the need arose they would be required
to move.

'My next one [move] *will be a
nursing home.'*

There would appear to be an argument for
greater clarity on this issue, so people know
where they are. Relatives particularly felt this.
Operational staff had a pragmatic view about
moves. A move to a nursing home or even
residential care because of dementia or
continual need for night cover did not
represent a failure to achieve objectives.
Housing managers, however, thought
otherwise. They felt that a move to residential
care was betraying the objectives of the
scheme.

To a tenant at Red Lodge there was a
subtle distinction between 'in' somewhere
and 'at' somewhere, the former denoting an
institution.

*'I am asked "How long have you been in
Red Lodge?" I say "I'm not in Red Lodge.
I am at Red Lodge".'*

On the residential side of Red Lodge, views
of institution/home were complex. Those
who had been admitted from the outside
community seem to see Red Lodge as
residential care but, as we shall see, not
as traditional residential care. The main
contributory factor in this quite positive
attitude seemed to be the relatively spacious
and attractive living quarters. Those who had
been living in Red Lodge as tenants and who
had undergone, not a physical transfer, but a
financial transfer from tenant to resident, felt
that their flat was their home.

High levels of satisfaction

Of the 16 City of York tenants individually
interviewed, 13 were very pleased they had
moved and 4 said they wished they had
moved earlier. They liked their flats, they liked
the social environment and they had a sense

of security and peace of mind. The fears they had had that what they might be moving to would be something like an institution were not realised. It is often observed that older people who move into 'provision' have no option but to be grateful to those who are looking after them. The qualitative interviewing used in this study seemed to allow people the opportunity to be frank and honest, and there were criticisms, as we shall see, of specific aspects of life in the schemes. It is possible, therefore, to be fairly confident that the move had proved to be, in overall terms, a positive experience. The three people who were not so enthusiastic were very similar to a typical resident in a care home in that they were resigned to, what to *them*, was inevitable.

Although they did not use the word, two or three of the Red Lodge residents did describe their living circumstances as relatively 'empowering' and very different from their idea of residential care with its rules and regulations. As just noted above, people's satisfaction seems to be as much to do with the 'housing nature' of their accommodation as with anything else. They very much liked their flats. They seem to like having others around them who are relatively independent. The sheltered tenants also were satisfied with their living situations but had some worries, as we see below, about increasing levels of disability in the scheme. The sheltered housing tenants received added value from the incorporation of residential care into the scheme. They benefited from the presence of the care staff and felt that their peace of mind had increased. Care staff, when making a cup of tea in a lounge for the residents on the care side, would also include tenants who happened to be there. It was this added value which worried the Registration and Inspection Unit because it felt it would detract from the care provided to the residents.

Independent living

The concept of independent living is a difficult one to research. It does not follow that, just because someone has their own front door, their independence is guaranteed. Moreover, providers' ideas of what independent living means are not always going to line up with an older person's. For example, in an evaluation of residential care, Oldman and Quilgars (1999) suggested that there could be considerable dissonance between older people's concept of independent living and professionals'. For example, the latter set great store on encouraging older people to do things for themselves. However, for some older people, going into provision does seem to represent a break from struggling. They indeed embrace the 'hotel model' of care which is anathema to some providers. They do not want to make their own bed. It is a comfortable feeling, having someone else whose wage you are paying do it for you.

In this study these attitudes were in evidence. Most people in the City of York schemes did want to maintain their independence and some hated having to wait for someone to come to their flat to push their wheelchair so they could get to the lift to go down to the dining room. But they also felt that the help that was available was their right and that it was a means to an end of achieving a better quality of life. The evaluation endorsed the research of Clark *et al* (1998) that 'dependent' older people do not particularly enjoy talking about the quality of care or care plans or care reviews. In this study, tenants/residents were much more animated about things other than care: about relationships, about getting on with the person who usually sits next to them at the meal table, about having enough to do during the day. Independent living meant being able to do things for oneself, but it also meant having some space, some social life that is your own and some independence from family members. Also, like Clark's older people, they preferred the word 'help' to the word 'care'.

People liked being able to get help. They felt that they could call the tune and say what it was they wanted help with.

> *'I just said I will have a bit of this and a bit of that.'*

They were very pleased with the staff who helped them.

> *'They are so pleasant.'*

There was evidence of some interesting negotiation.

> *'I don't need help dressing but – I know it's ridiculous – I can't get my tights on so they come in for that.'*

One worker said:

> *'She does the washing but we do the bending down to put it in the machine'.*

What most contributed to people's concept of independent living in both initiatives has already been touched upon: it was their feeling that they were living in their own home, not somebody's else. They could shut the door whenever they liked and they could be absolutely solitary if that was what they wanted. Nevertheless, independent living is also tied up with interactions from service providers and here, there were minor criticisms (dealt with in **Service provision**, page 48).

A final issue about independent living related to choice. It is very unlikely in residential care and also, although to a lesser extent, in community care for users to be able

to have wide choice about when to be got up, for example, or when to have breakfast. Both the initiatives tried hard to accommodate people's choices but only in a fairly limited way. However, the interviews show that people have quite low expectations – they were not very used to being able to choose!

Quality of life

The striking feature of the City of York schemes was the perception of a majority that their lives had greatly improved. In the timescale available to the research no attempt was made to measure health and welfare outcomes. Setting up a control group, as Keele University did in its research on Broadway Gardens in Wolverhampton, would have been contrary to the qualitative approach which had been adopted by this study. Instead, we took what people said to us at face value. We believed them when they said, as many did, that they had had a new lease of life, that their physical and mental health had improved and that they could do things now which they had not been able to do for some time. One woman said:

> *'I am a new woman now. People say they hardly recognise me!'*

People enjoyed living in what, for them, was quite clearly a vibrant community. A strong sense of supported housing as 'village' emerged. They also enjoyed their physical surroundings. Their housing circumstances were often an improvement on what they had had before. One person said:

> *'It is like living in a hotel permanently'.*

Some people said they had more, not less, space than before. One social services manager had a particular position on the built environment:

> *'I just think this building is fantastic. It is important in that it gives them a positive message. We are saying "We want you to live in a place like this which has cost a lot of money because you are worth it".'*

Just over a third of the City of York tenants said they now felt able or more confident to do things like cook a meal or have a shower which previously they had felt unable to do. This made them feel very good about themselves and was attributable to the more accessible built environment they were living in and the generally supportive atmosphere. There seemed to be quite a degree of mutual support.

On the contribution of physical design to quality of life, in one of the York schemes there were very some fairly trenchant criticisms. For some people the built environment was detracting from quality of life. Poor finishing-off and poor design for people with mobility problems were causing problems.

> *'Built and designed by men, of course. Why don't they consult us first?'*

The vibrancy of the schemes is difficult to explain. Some tenants themselves explained it in terms of the mix of people; some were relatively fit. One such tenant commented:

> *'We help one another. It's better for those with physical disabilities that they have got somebody to help them enjoy themselves as best they can. We've one or two who are a bit muddled but it's okay'.*

But some tenants were anxious about what they felt were increasing levels of frailty around them. They were concerned that in

a few years their schemes would look and feel like residential care.

> *'There are some here who shouldn't be.'*
>
> *'Some people are practically bedridden.'*
>
> *'They are all deaf. It gets on my nerves.'*

There were some worries that new people were coming in 'too late', that is, they were considered too frail. The tenants remarked that the original idea of having a mix of dependencies seemed to have been abandoned.

There was a degree of formal social activity in both initiatives, Red Lodge and the City of York schemes. To some degree this was organised by tenants. Some people flourished and joined in everything. Their relatives were sometimes a little startled. One said of her mother, a wheelchair user:

> *'I can't believe what's happening. She was a hermit. She seemed to hate people. Now she powers around the scheme joining in'.*

Some tenants had strong views that their schemes were communities that could be enjoyed.

> *'I am a people's person. I don't want to shut myself off as some people do when they get old.'*
>
> *'It is no good coming here and being miserable.'*

Others had a less enthusiastic attitude to the social side of things and kept out of the way.

The Red Lodge people were less ebullient about life, but there were some interesting themes. On the residential side, those people who were willing to discuss their situations felt that their quality of life had improved. They had a better social life than before, lived in fairly non-institutional surroundings and were not subject to obtrusive care. In the early days of the experiment the tenants had been a little hostile to the introduction of residential care. They felt easier about it when its dispersed nature changed and a dedicated wing was established. For the tenants, flexi-care had threatened the concept of sheltered housing as village. There is inevitable reluctance or unwillingness among older people to consider the possibility of future decline and helplessness. Being brought up close to the problems of old age through living 'cheek by jowl' with some people who may not be acting in a rational manner is not always a comfortable situation. It is difficult to say whether increasing the number of residential units will adversely affect the quality of life at Red Lodge. Some tenants did not seem too pleased about the proposals, which are at the behest of the Registration and Inspection Unit. However, when registration is fully complete it will still be a community where half the occupants have tenancies.

In **Chapter One** it was noted that very sheltered housing resources are increasingly being extended to the wider community. The day centre in Red Lodge was a community resource. Our findings support those of Tinker's (Royal Commission, 1999b Ch. 5) that tenants do not necessarily welcome such a development. It can, tenants feel, detract from a sense of community.

Service provision

From the viewpoint of the City of York tenants, the provision of care and support was very satisfactory. Earlier in the report it was suggested that, whether a provision is registered or not, the way care is delivered can be demeaning, ageist and disempowering. In the two schemes, however, none of this

seemed true. The principle of independence was adhered to. There was plenty of evidence that provision in both initiatives was flexible; people reported getting less/more care over time.

There were some fairly minor criticisms about service provision from the City of York tenants. In one scheme, tenants thought that the staff were '*rushed off their feet*' and as a consequence sometimes people felt they did not always get all the help they required. There were isolated examples of bossy staff, but generally tenants felt it was to be expected that you would not necessarily get on with everyone. Tenants and relatives alike, but the latter much more so, had concerns about the lack of night cover, but the strongest criticisms were reserved for the cooked-chilled midday meal.

There were some small criticisms of the care and support services. For example, people felt that the cleaning wasn't done that well and some people preferred to pay outsiders to do it. One City of York tenant was very disabled and required a great deal of help. However, all her help came from family members and indeed she paid one of her daughters a small wage. Others had help from the in-house team and paid for other help. In other schemes included in this study, this flexibility would not have been allowed. All care and support had to be provided by the scheme itself.

Although there was evidence that the City of York tenants felt they could say what help they wanted, nevertheless the formal care on offer was of the traditional variety. One woman received help from the scheme, but she also preferred to buy in additional care because she could dictate terms.

'Now it's summer what we do is, we clean for the first hour and then go into the park for the second and have a chat.'

This sort of flexibility is not a feature of formal care delivery patterns.

There was also some flexibility at Red Lodge. Some people were purchasing care privately and some from the care team. In the early days of the initiative, JRHT was competing against itself by providing residential and home care from the same source. In theory, at least, the same level of need could be supported either through home care or through residential care. It would be in people's financial interests to try and stay on the sheltered side. However, this has now changed with the Registration and Inspection Unit's insistence that the care package service should no longer remain unregistered.

The views reported above about care and support raise interesting issues. Both the initiatives were examples of integrated care and support, but it was apparent that people liked to be able to exercise some choice and receive services from others as well.

These findings about older people wanting to have choice over provider support other research. Parkinson and Pierpoint (2000) found that, where people were purchasing care privately, they were more satisfied because they could dictate terms more freely. Tenants in our schemes were generally very happy and they did like the in-house teams. However, there did, in this evaluation, appear to be some support for the separation of accommodation and care model. Tenants liked to be able to choose providers some-times. They could be a little more in control.

As well as the in-house team and/or private agencies, relatives were an important source of help and support. There is a considerable amount of literature on 'informal carers' – the term the social care profession use for relatives who support older and vulnerable people who live in the community. There is a very much smaller body of work about the role of relatives once

their family member has moved to residential care, and very little is known about the relatives' role once the older person has moved to sheltered housing. Wardens often assert that relatives 'give up' on the older person once the move has taken place (England *et al*, 2000). Evidence from both tenants and relatives in this study suggests that this is not so. Relatives were providing the whole spectrum of help from practical, emotional and social support through to, in some cases, intensive 'hands-on' caring which was making a massive contribution to avoiding a move to nursing or residential care. Costing studies need to acknowledge and build in the contribution of informal care.

The relatives in the study, who in the main were sons and daughters, were highly satisfied with the initiatives. Their lives had become easier in the sense that they no longer had two houses to look after (their own and the older person's) and caring was easier because the new accommodation was less disabling. They had secured a great deal more peace of mind as a result of the move and as a consequence felt that they could have a better, more relaxed relationship with their older person. Indeed, a number of people said they were now better able to go, as they put it, '*the last mile*'. It is this last point that needs to be taken up by providers. The relatives in the study did not feel they were expected to provide care and support, but they said they would like more information on an ongoing basis about the service provision. Very sheltered housing is new, and it is appropriate that providers begin to develop explicit relatives policies which suggest how a concept of partnership or 'shared care' would work. Care planning needs to include relatives' views and input.

Some of the relatives in the study were living in the schemes as spouses and chief carer of dependent tenants. A social work manager said that she believed that the capacity of the initiatives to provide for these situations had not particularly been anticipated. She was, however, delighted with the result. Couples were not being split up; in the absence of the schemes, residential care for the iller, more disabled partner would have been inevitable. Furthermore, a better quality of life had been secured for the less dependent partner; not only could they share the task of caring with the formal carers, but also they could benefit from the social aspects of living in a communal setting.

Tenants varied in their attitude to the relative. For some, a move to the scheme did represent more independence from relatives. They did not necessarily want a great deal of support from them. Others, however, preferred informal care to formal care.

The support workers in the City of York schemes and the care assistants at Red Lodge were interviewed. They all reported enjoying their jobs. Those in the City of York schemes who came from residential care backgrounds admitted that it was not easy delivering the sort of independent living which was expected of them. A minority did not like having to be cleaners as well as carers. Both the managers thought it was a key part of their team's job to devote time to non-caring tasks, such as the traditional warden job of popping in and talking to tenants. Both sets of care workers had difficult – because non-standard – jobs. The Red Lodge staff, for example, admitted to the stress of balancing the needs of the residents with those of tenants.

Affordability

In the main, the City of York schemes accommodate people who previously have rented. Allocation policies are still fundamentally housing-based and hence owner occupiers are not deemed to be in such need. However, it is recognised that this must change and, indeed, the schemes do have a small number of owner occupiers living in them. Here, affordability may be a problem. All the tenants except one who were interviewed were on Housing Benefit and/or Income Support. The one 'exception' had made his house over to his son within the required seven years. Everyone interviewed felt that both the rent and the care were affordable. However, for those whose incomes are above benefit levels, care and support can rise to £11 an hour in the City of York and so affordability may be a problem for people with heavy care needs.

As noted in the previous section, further research is needed on the financial contribution of informal care. The chapter has shown that relatives put in a lot of money and help. This may be making a difference to the affordabilty of provision.

Conclusions

This chapter has presented a pilot evaluation of York's innovative very sheltered schemes. It is described as pilot because there is, as yet, no consensus as to how evaluation of these hybrid forms of provision which are neither residential care nor sheltered housing should be approached. The study's qualitative methodology which centred on older people's accounts of their experience of moving into and living in the schemes suggested that, for the City of York schemes at least, the principal benefits conferred were improved quality of life and an enhanced feeling of both physical and psychological security. The JRHT scheme was also liked, but it was not comparable with the City of York schemes because the latter were brand new and were accommodating people who, due to their loneliness and poor health, had previously been living in quite difficult circumstances. It was perhaps to be expected that they would report high levels of satisfaction. They were quite pleased and, in a few cases, quite proud to be living in 'flagship' schemes.

The evaluation of the City of York scheme has shown that, not surprisingly, not all the stakeholders had the same views about the schemes. This may mean that the schemes are not achieving their full potential. Housing professionals who principally oversaw the allocation of places, in collaboration with social services, wanted the schemes to replace residential care. The social care side, by contrast, saw very sheltered housing not as a direct alternative but rather as adding to the options available to older people living in York. Both sets of professionals gave more prominence to quality of care than they did to quality of life. Although housing and social care professionals had rather different views of the initiative, nevertheless it probably would never have got off the ground if housing and social services had not been a single department. For the older people concerned, living in a vibrant community is more important than keeping out of residential care. However, their views are contradictory in the sense that they want an ordinary housing environment and, at the same time, night cover. They also want a home for life for themselves, but not for their neighbour with moderate dementia.

The City of York schemes which, in the classification provided in **Chapter Two**, were at the housing end, appeared to be having some success in providing a rehabilitative and 'preventative' environment, but at the expense of the managers' desire to 'divert from residential care'. Tenants wanted the original allocations policy of a balanced community maintained, but there is pressure on the Council to allocate a scarce resource to frailer people.

Red Lodge was very much more at the care end of the classification. What it set out to do was very innovative: the provision of registered care dispersed throughout the scheme. It was very successful in providing non-traditional residential care based on strong housing principles and it took away from its tenants the trauma of moving when care needs increase. However, there were problems. One of the attractive features of the original idea had been the notion that people could stay in their flats but become residents. Practical and management difficulties have resulted in abandonment of this dispersal feature in favour of a separate wing. Moreover, not all the stakeholders shared the same view of the initiative. The Registration and Inspection Unit was of the view that where highish levels of care are being delivered, registration should follow.

Finally, there were two common themes. One is what to do about relatives, who currently can be an important but perhaps unsung component of care and support. The other is the issue of affordability. Very sheltered housing is affordable because of its central link to Housing Benefit. But many older people who are not on Benefit may want to live in very sheltered housing.

Chapter Six
Conclusions

The key finding of this study of communal living arrangements for older people is that they are not necessarily a negative experience. Age-segregated environments can, in certain circumstances, be actively sought and can produce a better quality of life than that experienced before the move. They may also, for some people, have a recuperative effect and/or prolong their healthy years a little. However, the opportunities in Britain at present for this sort of lifestyle are very limited indeed and are only available to those who have substantial financial resources. Rather, access to communal living, whether in housing or in care schemes, is subject to allocation criteria which place priority on dependency levels and issues of cost-effectiveness. Where it is considered that it is uneconomic to care for an older person in their own home, a move may be recommended. The social or collective needs of older people tend not be given emphasis in allocation and assessment procedures. The report has reviewed models of provision which are neither residential care nor sheltered housing but which are predicated on the assumption that having 'your own front door', having housing rights, results in a more empowering experience than the much disliked dependent living which for so long has been associated with residential care. The limited fieldwork with older people carried out for this study suggests this may be right. Very sheltered housing seems to be a place to live in rather than a place to die in. The principles of independent living do have a better chance of becoming a reality in housing schemes where everyone has their 'own front door'.

A number of policy issues are emerging from the study; they deserve some attention so that very sheltered housing can play its proper part in the new preventative agenda for community care. However, before these are explored, a case is made here for a change in terminology. Throughout this report, for simplicity's sake, the term 'very sheltered housing' has been used to describe all the different models which have emerged recently which are neither unambiguously residential care nor unambiguously sheltered housing. A suggestion is made that the term 'supported housing' be used instead. Such a change seems to suit the new paradigm of later life, one in which older people are more empowered, more able to achieve independent living. The old terms – very sheltered housing, assisted living, close care and all the rest – seem to focus on the 'special' nature of old age and on the idea of dependency.

The report has shown that the boundaries between housing provision and care provision are becoming blurred. It has also shown that models based on the principle of your own front door are alternatives to traditional residential care. This is an exciting time to be contemplating new and attractive living arrangements for older people. The Royal Commission, for example, raises the possibility of residential care for purchase. It notes, in passing, the idea that residents might purchase a lease on an accommodation unit which can be sold after death, in line with some developments in Denmark. It was noted in **Chapter One** of this report that, in an important lecture, *Living in Someone Else's Home* (1997), Clough called for an end to the system of residential care as we have it now, whereby people occupy a room on a lump-sum, weekly-fee basis. It should, he argued, be replaced by a system whereby people rent or own their living space and care is delivered to them. However, there are some major policy obstacles to 'your own front door' becoming a widespread reality. The most central of these is the present uneasy juxtaposition of registration/regulation and funding.

The report has shown that, although the boundaries between residential care and the newer forms of supported housing provision for older people are blurring in terms of their purpose and in terms of whom they accommodate, there are, nevertheless, two structural systems of provision, one 'care' and one 'housing', which produce different outcomes for those who live in them. The first are registered, currently under the *Residential Homes Act* and, soon, under the *Care Standards Act*. Residents pay a 'blanket' fee which, although paid by different 'bits' of the social policy system, rolls up accommodation, living costs and care costs. Residents have no housing rights and hence do not receive housing and other benefits. In supported housing for older people, although the agencies delivering care will, in 2002, have to be registered, the accommodation will generally *not* be registered. Tenants pay separately for their accommodation, living costs and care. This allows for much more flexibility than that which pertains in the residential care situation. Care and support can be more carefully matched to people's needs and wants. It can reduce as well as increase, and people have more opportunity to exercise choice and control over what they

get. Finally, and most importantly, in supported housing people are usually better off financially because their access to housing and other benefits means that their disposable income after housing and support costs have been paid is higher than that of the typical person living in residential care.

This report's central recommendation, thus, is that issues of registration and the issues of funding should be decoupled. In the next two years, before the setting up of the new National Care Standards Commission, there will be time for a further look at different approaches to registration and regulation in different settings. This report has suggested that, although quantifiable issues like numbers of fire exits and staffing levels are absolutely essential in standard-setting, there needs to be more of a focus on quality of life and principles of independent living. Supported housing providers should not have to fear registration. Rather, they might welcome it, but only if the link between registration and funding is broken so that registration does not threaten independent living by ending people's housing status and access to Housing Benefit.

There seems to be a strong case for moving over to a uniform funding system which charges separately for:

- accommodation
- living costs
- care and support.

This would blur the boundaries between housing and care further, allow for a range of different models and make 'your own front door' a reality for all older people living in all types of communal arrangements. It would also make more possible what this report has shown older people want – balanced communities with a range of dependency levels and a focus on quality of life.

Quite clearly, for the decoupling of registration and funding to come to pass, more information is needed on costs and in particular on:

- the variation in capital costs
- the variation in revenue costs
- affordability
- the contribution of informal care.

We also do not know much about cost-effectiveness. The report has suggested that supported housing for older people is not usually cheaper in resource costs than either residential care or intensive home support, but it has begun to produce some evidence that the different supported housing models confer enhanced quality of life and can make a contribution to preventative community care. What is needed is a financial modelling exercise which looks at the consequences for the public purse of charging separately for accommodation, living costs and care in all communal settings for older people

There are problems with the current funding system. First, there is a **dearth of capital funding** for supported housing for older people and yet there are opportunities to revisit old ideas. In 1986 the Joseph Rowntree Housing Trust pioneered 'flexible tenure' (Joseph Rowntree Memorial Trust, 1990), a mixed-tenure model which allowed people to 'staircase down' as well as up (sell proportions of housing equity). Its aim was to increase the supply of housing for older people by drawing in their personal finance (usually housing equity) alongside the usual subsidies. It floundered only because of bureaucratic intransigence evident at the time due to the difficulty of mixing public and private finance. It seems its time has now come. There is now much more evidence that older people possess significant amounts of housing equity and that at present, if they seek out supported housing to purchase, there are very limited opportunities. Also, the financial climate might now be more

welcoming towards public/private funding initiatives.

There are also difficulties on the revenue side. In 2003 the new policy for funding supported housing comes in. Providers in this study thought it was quite difficult to predict the effects of *Supporting People*. The amount of money involved is small. Respondents thought that around £15 per person represents the sort of amount for support services that will come out of the entitlement-based Housing Benefit system and go into the new grant to be administered by local authorities. The more significant problem may be Housing Benefit officers' attitudes to high rents and the whole future of Housing Benefit. *Supporting People* may be a threat. Local authorities may not be prepared to fund the support element, on the grounds that such support may discriminate against the majority of older people living in the community. However, this and other research suggests that it is the low-level support delivered in the past by wardens which is highly valued by older people. Although most existing supported housing schemes for older people are probably going to be fairly secure after 2003, there must be some anxiety about local authorities' attitudes to commissioning communal living. In addition, the avowed intention of *Supporting People* is to blur the division between housing, care and support. There is very little evidence that current demarcation disputes about what activity falls under which heading – and which agency should pay – will end.

Finally, we must return to older people. They must be brought into the debate about 'your own front door'. The Royal Commission found that they were confused about the difference between sheltered housing and residential care. There is little information on their views on the use of housing wealth to buy into communal settings, the use of Direct

Payments with which people can buy what care and support they want, and on different care and support organisational models. This report suggests that older people would prefer service delivery to move away from its mainly medical perspective to a social model – one which focuses not on impairment but on need. Service delivery is still covertly or even overtly ageist, and employs assessment practices which largely exclude older people. The latter seem to want choice and control – when to move to communal settings, when to get up and when to go to bed. They seem to want help, not care.

References

Age Concern (1998) *Beyond Bricks and Mortar: Dignity and security in the home.* Submission by Age Concern to the Royal Commission on Long Term Care for the Elderly. Policy Papers 1398.

Audit Commission (1996) *Balancing the Care Equation.* London: Audit Commission.

Audit Commission (1997) *The Coming of Age: Improving care services for older people.* London: Audit Commission.

Audit Commission (1998) *Home Alone: The role of housing in community care.* London: Audit Commission.

Bailey, A. (1998) Making God wait: an alternative to residential care. *Housing Care and Support* **1** (2).

Baldock, J. (1997) More than a funding problem. *Social Policy and Administration* **31** (1) 73–89.

Baldwin, N., Harris, L. & Kelly, D. (1993) Institutionalisation: why blame the institution? *Ageing and Society* **13** (1) 69–81.

Bartholomeou, J. A. (1999) *View of the Future: The Experience of Living in ExtraCare.* Staines: Hanover Housing Group.

Brenton, M. (1998) '*We're in Charge': Co-housing communities of older people in The Netherlands: Lessons for Britain?* Bristol: The Policy Press.

Butler, A., Oldman, C. & Greve, J. (1983) *Sheltered Housing for the Elderly: Policy, practice and the consumer.* London: Allen and Unwin.

Cebulla, A. with Beach, J., Heaver, C., Irving, Z., Walker, R. & the National Centre for Social Research (1999) *Housing Benefit and Supported Accommodation.* Department of Social Security Research Report No. 93. Leeds: Corporate Document Services.

Clapham, D. (1997) Problems and potential of sheltered housing. *Ageing and Society* **17** (2) 209–214.

Clapham, D. & Munro, M. (1988) *A Comparison of Sheltered and Amenity Housing for Older People.* Edinburgh: Scottish Office.

Clapham, D. & Munro, M. (1990) Ambiguities and contradiction in the provision of sheltered housing for older people. *Journal of Social Policy* **19** (1) 27–45.

Clapham, D., Munro, M. & Kay, H. (1994) *A Wider Choice: Revenue funding mechanisms for housing and community care.* York: Joseph Rowntree Foundation.

Clark, H., Dyer, S. & Horwood, J. (1998) *That Bit of Help.* Bristol: The Policy Press.

Clough, R. (1997) *Living in Someone Else's Home: The concept of negotiation, the process of ownership and the role of relationships in homes for older people.* London: Counsel and Care.

Cooper, L., Watson, L. & Allen, G. (1994) *Shared Living: Social relations in supported housing.* Social Services Monographs: Research in practice. Sheffield: University of Sheffield, Joint Unit for Social Services Research and Community Care.

Davies, B., Bebbington, A. & Charnley, H. (1990) *Resources, Needs and Outcomes in Community-Based Care.* Aldershot: Avebury.

Department of Health (1989) *Caring for People: Community care in the next decade and beyond.* London: HMSO.

Department of Health (1997) *Better Services for Vulnerable People.* London: Department of Health.

Department of Health (1998a) *Modernising Social Services: Promoting independence, improving protection and raising standards.* London: The Stationery Office.

Department of Health (1998b) *Better Services for Vulnerable People: Maintain the momentum.* London: Department of Health.

Department of Health (1998c) *Partnership in Action: New opportunities for joint working between health and social services.* London: Department of Health.

Department of Health (1999) *Fit for the Future? Nationally Required Standards for Residential and Nursing Care.* London: Department of Health.

Department of Social Security (1998) *Supporting People: A policy and funding framework for support services.* London: Department of Social Services.

England, J., Oldman, C. & Hearnshaw, S. (2000) *A Question of Shared Care? The Role of Relatives in Sheltered Housing.* Oxford: Anchor Trust.

Evandrou, M. (1997) *Baby Boomers: Ageing in the 21st Century.* London: Age Concern.

Fletcher, P., Riseborough, M., Humphries, J., Jenkins, C. & Whittingham, P. (1999) *Citizenship and Services in Older Age: The strategic role of very sheltered housing.* Beaconsfield: Housing 21.

Gavilan, H. (1992) Care in the community: issues of dependency and control: the similarities between institution and home. *Generations Review* **2** (4) 9–11 14.

Gibbs, I. & Wright, K. (1993) *Anchor Care Team: An appraisal.* Oxford: Anchor Trust.

Goss, S. (1998) *A Framework for Housing with Support: A tool to describe, evaluate and continuously improve services.* London: National Housing Federation.

Greenwood, C. & Smith, J. (1999) *Sharing in ExtraCare.* Staines: Hanover Housing Group.

Griffiths, S. (1997) *Housing Benefit and Supported Accommodation: The implications of recent changes.* York: York Publishing Services.

Gubrium, J. (1993) *Speaking of Life: Horizons of meaning for nursing home residents.* New York: Aldine de Gruyter.

Hancock, R. (2000) Estimating the housing wealth of older home owners. *Housing Studies* **15** (4) 553–579.

Harrison, L. & Heywood, F. (2000) *Health Begins at Home: Planning at the health–housing interface.* Bristol: The Policy Press.

Hasler, J. & Page, D. (1998) *Sheltered Housing is Changing: The Emerging Role of the Warden.* Nottingham: Metropolitan Housing Trust.

Higgins, J. (1989) Defining community care: realities and myths. *Social Policy and Administration* **23** (2) 3–16.

Joseph Rowntree Memorial Trust (1990) *Flexible Tenure: Lessons learned from an innovative housing project for elderly people.* York: JRMT.

Kitwood, T., Buckland, S. & Petre, T. (1995) *Brighter Homes: A Report on Research into Provision for Persons with Dementia in Residential Homes, Nursing Homes and Sheltered Housing.* Oxford: Anchor Housing Association.

Laing and Buisson (1998) *Care of Elderly People: Market Survey,* 11th edn. London: Laing and Buisson.

McCafferty, P. (1994) *Living Independently: A study of the housing needs of elderly and disabled people.* London: HMSO.

Marsh, A. & Riseborough, M. (1995) *Making Ends Meet: Older people, housing costs and the affordability of rented housing.* London: National Federation of Housing Association.

Middleton, L. (1981) *So Much for So Few: A view of sheltered housing.* Liverpool: Institute of Human Ageing, University Of Liverpool.

Neill, J., Sinclair, I., Gorbach, P. & Williams, J. (1988) *A Need for Care: Elderly applicants for local authority homes.* Aldershot: Gower.

Netten, A. & Dennett, J. (1997) *Unit Costs of Health and Social Care.* Canterbury: Personal Social Services Unit, University of Kent.

Netten, A., Bebbington, A., Darton, R., Forder, J. & Miles, K. (1998) *Survey of Care Homes for Elderly People.* Final Report. Kent: PSSRU.

Nocon, A. & Pleace, N. (1999) Sheltered housing and community care. *Social Policy and Administration* **23** (2) 164–180.

Oldman, C. (1991) Financial effects of moving in old age. *Housing Studies* **6** (4) 251–262.

Oldman, C. (1998) *Incorporating Residential Care into Sheltered Housing: The Red Lodge experiment.* York: Centre for Housing Policy, University of York.

Oldman, C. & Pleace, N. (1993) Residential care in a housing setting. *Regional Review* **3** (3) 3.

Oldman, C. & Pleace, N. (1995) The over-lapping boundaries between housing and care: the case of frail older people in housing schemes. *Housing Review* May/June 59–60.

Oldman, C., Quilgars, D. & Oldfield, N. (1996) *Housing Benefit and Service Charges*. London: The Stationery Office.

Oldman, C., Quilgars, D. & Carlisle, J. (1997) *Living in a Home: The experience of living and working in residential care in the 1990s*. Oxford: Anchor Trust.

Oldman, C. & Quilgars, D. (1999) The last resort? Revisiting ideas about older people's living arrangements. *Ageing and Society* **19** (4) 363–384.

Parkinson, P. & Pierpoint, D. (2000) *Preventative Approaches in Housing: An exploration of good practice*. Oxford: Anchor Trust.

Peace, S., Kellaher, L. & Willcocks, D. (1997) *Re-evaluating Residential Care*. Buckingham: Open University Press.

Phillips, M. (1998) Modelling course. *Housing Today* 4th November 18–19.

Plank, D. (1977) *Caring for the Elderly: Report of a study of caring for dependent elderly people in eight London boroughs*. London: Greater London Council.

Quilgars, D. (2000) *Low Intensity Support Services: A systematic review*. Bristol: Policy Press.

Raynes, N. (1999) Older residents' participation in specifying quality in nursing and residential homes. *Generations Review* **9** (2) 10–12.

Reed, J. & Payton, V. (1996) Constructing familiarity and managing self: ways of adapting to life in nursing and residential homes for older people. *Ageing and Society* **16** (5) 543–60.

Robson, D., Nicholson, A. M. & Barker, N. (1997) *Homes for the Third Age: A design guide for extra care sheltered housing*. London: Spon.

Royal Commission on Long Term Care (1999a) *With Respect to Old Age: Long term care – rights and responsibilities*. Cm 4192–I. London: The Stationery Office.

Royal Commission on Long Term Care (1999b) *Alternative Models of Care for Older People*. Royal Commission on Long Term Care Research Vol. 2. Cm 4192–II/2. London: The Stationery Office.

Rummery, K. & Glendinning, C. (1999) Negotiating needs, access and gatekeeping. *Critical Social Policy* **19** (3) 335–354.

Simons, K. (1998) The regulation of housing and support services. *Housing Care and Support* **1** (3).

Seymour, P. (1997) *Evaluation of Somerville Very Sheltered Housing Scheme*. Lewisham Social Services.

Thompson, D. & Page, D. (1999) *Effective Sheltered Housing: A good practice guide*. London: Chartered Institute of Housing.

Tinker, A. (1989) *An Evaluation of Very Sheltered Housing*. London: HMSO.

Tinker, A., Wright, F. & Zeilig, H. (1995) *Difficult to Let Sheltered Housing*. London: HMSO.

Townsend, P. (1962) *The Last Refuge*. London: Routledge and Kegan Paul.

Trotter, E. & Phillips, M. (1997) *Remodelling Sheltered Housing*. Beaconsfield: Housing 21.

Twigg, J. (1997) Deconstructing the 'social bath': help with bathing at home for old and disabled people. *Journal of Social Policy* **26** (2) 211–32.

Wilcocks, D., Peace, S. & Kellaher, L. (1987) *Private Lives in Public Places: A research-based critique of residential care in local authority old people's homes*. London: Tavistock Publications.

Woolham, J. (1998) *Very Sheltered Housing: A study of its impact and effectiveness in meeting the housing and social care needs of older people*. Northamptonshire County Council, Policy Division.

Appendix A
Topic guide for providers

The major providers

How many 'ordinary' sheltered schemes do you have?

....

How many 'very sheltered' schemes do you have?

....

How do you define the latter? Please describe what it looks like. What different variants of very sheltered housing do you have?

....

....

....

....

....

....

....

....

Are any very sheltered schemes registered under the *Residential Homes Act*?

....

....

If provider does develop very sheltered schemes, why?

....

....

....

If no formalised very sheltered schemes, how do you approach the issue of 'home for life'?

☐ modify the physical environment

☐ provide in-house care to selected tenants in ordinary schemes

☐ have formal care agreements with social services

☐ try to get home care for tenants

☐ expect people to move on to residential care

☐ other

If no very sheltered housing, why?

....

....

....

....

....

....

How explicit are you to relatives, older people and others about the limits, if any, of your provision? Are there publicly available policies?

....

....

....

....

What services are provided in either your sheltered or your very sheltered schemes?

☐ getting up in the morning/going to bed at night service

☐ cooking

☐ meal provision

☐ cleaning

☐ shopping

☐ 24-hour care

☐ laundry

☐ formal social activity

☐ other

● Discuss the source and mix of provider of all these different services: social services on formal contract or otherwise; in-house provider; residential or peripatetic; relatives; privately purchased by user etc.

● Discuss why different arrangements prevail.

● If provider has both very sheltered housing schemes and sheltered schemes, what plans does it have concerning the latter in terms of 'home for life'?

....

....

....

....

....

....

● Discuss mission statements or aims and objectives, if available, of the different models which have emerged.

● Discuss different sources of income available to users to pay for services.

● Discuss income and capital diversity of residents.

● Discuss rent and service charge levels; can they send breakdowns? What component of the rent is eligible rent? Roughly what percentage of tenants are on Housing Benefit?

● If it has not come up in the discussion thus far, discuss the issue of physical design and barrier-free environments: assisted bathing, lifts, wheelchair units etc.

● Are you a residential care provider? Discuss relationship of this provision to housing provision.

Are you providing any other models such as shared housing, halfway house, hostel for older people, which we haven't yet mentioned?

....

....

....

How do you approach the evaluation of your different schemes and models?

....

....

....

What about the future? Are you going to do more or less of the above and why?

....

....

....

Are *Supporting People* and *Modernising Social Services* significant documents for you?

....

....

....

Do you know of any other interesting models in this area which others might be doing or are considering?

....

....

....

....

....

Appendix B
Topic guide for tenants

Welcome/introduction/thanks; confidentiality, purpose of meeting (assessing innovation), independence of research, no right/wrong answers.

Coming here

- How long have you been here? What were the reasons for your moving here?

- Degree of commitment/reluctance to decide to move, positive/negative attitude to previous home, positive/negative attitude to move, whose decision is it, involvement in decision, role of financial factors in move, other options/alternatives

- Immediate antecedents of move; understanding of the assessment process

- Life before, where, what tenure and degree of help and support from various sources, formal and informal; where immediately before moving on to scheme

- What did you think it was going to be like? Has it met/exceeded expectations? Did you think it was going to be like residential care? Explore any change for better or worse in health/wellbeing

What sort of place

- What do you call this place? What do you say it is?

- What do you call yourselves (tenants/residents)?

- What is your understanding of your security of tenure? Probe home for life concept

- In what ways is it different from living at home? What things are good/bad compared with home?

The physical environment

What do you think about your flat here?

- assess degree of accessibility

- space

- attractiveness

What about the scheme generally? What do you think of it?

- location

- ambience/atmosphere; temperature; public areas; design

People

What about the people here, the other tenants, the staff, people who visit regularly?

- other tenants, friendships, mutual support, attitudes to disability; did you know anyone before?

- frequency of contacts with relatives and friends

- what are the staff like?

Social aspects of living in the scheme

What about the social side of things here?

- picking up on previous questions; better/worse quality of social life before; possibilities of getting out better/worse/same, not an issue

- views on organised social activity

- do you tenants have any involvement in running the place?

Everyday life

Just run through a typical day here for me. Have you got:

- enough to do?

- care and support delivery?

Services

Are you getting services from the team of helpers here? What do you think of those services?

- Did you decide what help you get? Explore process of assessment

- Do you have the midday meal? What is it like? What do you do for your other meals?

- Has the degree and nature of help you get changed since you moved in?

- Tenant/staff relationships; independence, empowerment, ageism

- Do you get enough help/too much help?

- Help from other sources; other formal, families, each other

Financial

Let's move on to how much it costs to live here. What do you have to pay for rent, for care/support? About how much is it costing you to live here, for everything – food, utilities, leisure and so on?

- Do you think you get value for money?

- Gauge views on affordability

- Distinguish between affordability of rent and affordability of care

- Degree of help provided by informal carers (from question above)

Closing

So, in drawing it to a close, let's recap: what's good about being here? What's bad about being here?

- Would you recommend it to others?

THANK YOU VERY MUCH

Appendix C

Organisations consulted

- Abbeyfield Society
- Anchor Trust
- City of York Council
- Elderly Accommodation Council
- Extra Care Charitable Trust
- Hanover Housing Group
- Housing 21
- Joseph Rowntree Housing Trust
- Lewisham Social Services
- National Housing Federation
- Northamptonshire Social Services